# food

# cook

# eat

# food
# cook
# eat

## lulu grimes

**MURDOCH**
**B O O K S**

# contents

# how to start

This book is for people who like eating nice food, nothing complicated, just the kind of dishes you might choose when eating out at a local restaurant. That is to say, these are tried and trusted recipes, comforting and, in the most part, familiar — the kind of food you want to eat every day just because it is yummy.

These recipes are not long-winded and won't take forever at the end of a hard day's work. Some recipes have the odd ingredient that you might have to search for but most can be put together from your local supermarket or high street shop. Cooking times vary — some dishes require a little time to prepare and have a short cooking time, others can be thrown together and then left to cook for a while.

Recipes are located in chapters according to the main ingredient in each dish, so you can easily find a recipe based on something you may already have in the fridge or cupboard should you so choose. Ingredients are listed first, followed by the amount you need and then preparation instructions, where applicable.

Most of the recipes serve two people reasonably generously, with larger dishes such as roasts serving four. If you want to make anything for a bigger group of people, simply double things up.

That's it really. Provided your oven, grill and cooktop are in working order and you have the basic equipment listed on the next page, you are ready to go.

## What every kitchen needs:

If you haven't got a well-stocked kitchen, don't worry, you don't need a huge amount of equipment to get started.

Essentially you will need:
* a large knife for chopping, a small knife for paring and peeling, and a serrated knife for cutting bread

* a large chopping board

* a large saucepan for pasta and potatoes, a small saucepan for everything else, and a casserole dish with a lid, which can double as an extra saucepan if you need it to

* a frying pan with a handle that will go in the oven or under the grill without melting

* a couple of wooden spoons, a rubber scraper, a cheese grater, a potato peeler, a slotted spoon, a potato masher (a grid-shaped one) and a fish slice

* a couple of baking dishes, a roasting tin and a flat oven tray.

As well, you will need the following assorted equipment:
* a blender
* a lemon squeezer
* a couple of glass or metal bowls for mixing
* some electric beaters or a wire whisk and muscle power
* a colander for draining
* a timer (essential if you get easily sidetracked)
* weighing scales, a measuring jug and cup measures
* a decent corkscrew and tin opener — cheap ones never ever work as well.

## Why eggs?

Eggs are a versatile, highly nutritious food (the yolk contains more protein than the white) and are incredibly easy to cook in a variety of ways. If you have a box of eggs in the fridge, you'll never go hungry!

## What to look for:

Choose eggs that are as fresh as possible. Egg boxes, and sometimes the eggs themselves, have dates stamped on them which refer either to the day they are laid or a use-by date. If you buy fresh eggs, they will last for a week.

* When eggs are fresh, they have a much more gelatinous white, which makes them easier to poach and fry. Slightly older eggs (2 to 3 days or more) are easier to whisk and to peel when boiled.

* To check the freshness of an egg, lower it into a bowl of water. A fresh egg will lie horizontally at the bottom but a stale egg will stand upright, held up by the air bubble that has formed inside it.

## What's available?

Free-range eggs are generally healthier but just what constitutes a free-range, barn-laid or organic egg can vary from country to country. Find organic free-range eggs if you can as they will have been laid by the happiest chickens. You can use anything from hen eggs to ostrich eggs, if you choose — the ones listed below are the most commonly available.

* Hen eggs can be brown or white: the colour makes no difference to the flavour. Hen eggs are available in sizes 1 (70 g) to 7 (45 g), with the standard sized eggs being size 3 (60 g). Double yolk eggs are just as they are described and sometimes you can buy boxes of these.

* Quail eggs are tiny speckled eggs that can be cooked like hen eggs, though for a shorter time (2 to 3 minutes).

* Duck eggs, which are larger than hen eggs and have a pale blue or white shell, can be used in baking and other cooking.

# eggs benedict

eggs  6, straight from the fridge

prosciutto  2 slices

English muffins  2

butter  110 g (4 oz)

lemon juice  1 tablespoon

serves  2    takes  15 minutes

1 Turn on the grill. Put a large frying pan full of water over a high heat. When the water is bubbling, turn the heat down to a gentle simmer. Crack an egg into a cup and slip the egg gently into the water. The egg should start to turn opaque almost as soon as it hits the water. Do the same with 3 more eggs, keeping them separated. Don't worry if the eggs spread out in the water. Turn the heat down as low as you can and leave the eggs for 3 minutes.

2 Put the prosciutto on a baking tray, put it under the grill for 2 minutes, then turn it over and cook the other side. Put the muffins in a toaster or under the grill to toast.

3 Crack the remaining eggs into a blender, put the lid on and leave the top hole open. Heat the butter in a small pan, or in the microwave, until it has completely melted and is bubbling. This will only take a minute or so in a pan. Be careful not to let it brown.

4 Start the blender and pour in the bubbling butter in a steady stream through the top hole. The eggs should thicken straight away to make a thick sauce. Add the lemon juice and season the hollandaise with salt and black pepper.

5 Put the muffins on individual plates and put a slice of prosciutto on each. Carefully lift each egg out of the water using a slotted spoon, drain briefly and put them on top of the prosciutto. Spoon some hollandaise over each egg.

Making hollandaise sauce and poaching eggs at the same time, or even at all, may seem daunting, but both tasks are actually very easy. Use smoked salmon instead of prosciutto if you like.

These Mexican-style breakfast eggs, which have a kick to them, are perfect for brunches or even suppers. If you like very hot food, add another chilli or a shake of Tabasco.

# huevos rancheros

olive oil  1 tablespoon

small white onion  1 finely chopped

green capsicum (pepper)  1/2 finely chopped

red chilli  1 finely chopped

garlic clove  1 crushed

dried oregano  1/2 teaspoon

tomato  1 chopped

tinned chopped tomatoes  400 g (14 oz)

eggs  4

flour tortillas  2

feta cheese  50 g (1/3 cup) crumbled

serves  2  takes  25 minutes

1 Put the olive oil in a frying pan (one with a lid) over a medium heat. Add the onion and green capsicum and fry them gently together for 2 minutes, or until they are soft.

2 Add the chilli and garlic and stir briefly, then add the oregano, fresh and tinned tomatoes, and 90 ml (3 fl oz) water. Bring to the boil, then turn down the heat and simmer gently for 5 minutes, or until the sauce thickens. Season with salt and pepper.

3 Smooth the surface of the mixture, then make four hollows with the back of a spoon. Break an egg into each hollow and put the lid on the pan. Cook the eggs for 5 minutes, or until they are set.

4 While the eggs are cooking, heat the tortillas according to the instructions on the packet and cut each into quarters.

5 Serve the eggs with some feta crumbled over them and the tortillas on the side.

# spanish omelette with smoked salmon

olive oil 1 tablespoon

potatoes 200 g (7 oz) peeled and cubed

small onion 1 finely chopped

eggs 4

dill 1 tablespoon chopped

smoked salmon 4 slices

mascarpone cheese 2 tablespoons

salad leaves 2 handfuls

serves 2 takes 20 minutes

1 Heat the oil in a small non-stick frying pan and add the potato cubes. Fry them gently, stirring them so they brown on all sides and cook through to the middle. Depending on how big your pieces of potato are, this will take about 10 minutes. Cut a cube open to see if they are cooked through completely.

2 When the potato is cooked, add the onion and cook it gently for a few minutes. You need to cook it until it is translucent and soft. Switch on the grill.

3 When the onion is almost ready, break the eggs into a bowl and whisk them together with some salt and pepper and the dill.

4 Tear the smoked salmon into pieces and add it to the frying pan. Add the mascarpone in blobs. Using a spatula, pull the mixture into the centre of the pan and level it off. Pour the eggs over the top and cook for 4 minutes, or until the omelette is just set.

5 Put the frying pan under the grill for a minute to lightly brown the top of the omelette.

6 Slide the omelette out of the frying pan and cut it into four wedges. Arrange a handful of salad leaves on each plate and top with two wedges of omelette.

This more substantial type of omelette makes a really good lunch or supper dish served with a salad and bread. Make sure you don't overcook the eggs or they will go slightly rubbery. The ideal omelette is slightly creamy in the centre.

These breakfast tarts involve making pastry, but if you prefer, you can buy ready-made shortcrust pastry. For a vegetarian version, add some chopped baby spinach leaves instead of the ham.

# breakfast tarts

plain (all-purpose) flour  220 g
(1³/₄ cups)

butter  140 g (5 oz), straight from
the fridge and diced

eggs  5

ham  2 slices

parsley  1 tablespoon chopped

medium tomato  1 finely chopped

cream  3 tablespoons

Parmesan cheese  2 tablespoons
grated

serves 2  takes 40 minutes

1 Turn the oven on to 200°C (400°F/Gas 6). Sift the flour and ¹/₂ teaspoon of salt into a food processor, add the butter and process for a few seconds until the mixture resembles breadcrumbs. Alternatively, rub the butter into the flour in a bowl. Add an egg and enough water (2 to 3 teaspoons) to make the mixture come together when you either process it briefly or mix it together using a palette knife. Bring the dough together using your hands and shape into two balls. Wrap both balls in plastic wrap and put one of them in the fridge for 10 minutes. Put the other ball in the freezer to use at another time.

2 Roll the pastry out on a floured work surface until it is very thin. Cut out two 16 cm (6¹/₂ inch) circles and use them to line two 10 cm (4 inch) tartlet tins. Press the pastry gently into the flutes of the tins. Don't worry if the pastry sticks up just above the tin. Line each tin with a piece of crumpled greaseproof paper and some uncooked rice. Bake the pastry for 5 minutes, then take out the paper and rice and bake for another minute.

3 Line each pastry base with the ham (you may need to cut it into pieces to make it fit neatly). Sprinkle with the parsley and add the tomato. Gently break two eggs into each tin, then pour half of the cream over the top of each, sprinkle with Parmesan and dust with salt and pepper.

4 Put the tarts in the oven and bake for 10 to 12 minutes, or until the egg whites are set. Serve hot or cold.

This recipe uses lavash breads, but if you can't get them, you can use Lebanese or Greek flatbreads, or stuff the mixture into pitta pockets. The red onion and capsicum mixture also goes well with leftover roast chicken or meat.

# fried egg and red onion wrap

olive oil   1 tablespoon

red onions   2 thickly sliced

red capsicum (pepper)   1 sliced

balsamic vinegar   $1/2$ tablespoon

eggs   2

lavash breads   2

sour cream   2 tablespoons

sweet chilli sauce

serves 2   takes 15 minutes

1 Heat the olive oil in a non-stick frying pan and add the onion. Cook it slowly, stirring occasionally until it softens and turns translucent. Add the red capsicum and continue cooking until both the onion and capsicum are soft. Turn the heat up and stir for a minute or two, or until they start to brown, then stir in the balsamic vinegar.

2 Push the mixture over to one side of the pan and carefully break both eggs into the other side, keeping them separate if you can. Cook over a gentle heat until the eggs are just set.

3 Heat the lavash breads in a microwave or under a grill for a few seconds (you want them to be soft and warm). Lay the breads out on a board, spread a tablespoon of sour cream onto the centre of each, then drizzle with a little chilli sauce. Put a heap of the onion and capsicum mixture on each and top with an egg. Season with salt and pepper.

4 Fold in one short end of each piece of lavash bread and then roll each one up lengthways. This will help prevent the filling from falling out as you eat.

# bacon and sausages

## Why bacon?

Depending on how bacon is cured, it can be salty or sweet, and smoked or unsmoked. Bacon is useful both as a main ingredient and as a flavouring. Even if you only have one rasher of bacon in your fridge, you can use it to add lots of flavour to a soup, salad or pasta sauce.

## What to look for:

Bacon should look fairly dry with a sheen on its surface. Its fat should be a creamy colour and feel solid. Packaged bacon is often very wet so buy loose rashers if possible.

## What's available?

Bacon is sold with or without the rind — the choice is yours.

* Back bacon is sold as rashers and chops.

* Streaky bacon has a high percentage of fat to meat and crisps up well.

* Gammon is leg meat, cured like bacon. It has a milder flavour than ham and is usually sold as a joint or cut into steaks.

* Canadian bacon, good for breakfast, has a sweet flavour and very little fat.

* Speck is the German word for bacon. It comes in slabs and slices.

* Pancetta is Italian salt-cured pork belly, which comes smoked and unsmoked, in slices, slabs or cubes.

## Why sausages?

Sausages can be eaten as the main part of the meal or chopped up to use as an ingredient.

## What to look for:

Buy sausages that look as if they have been made from meat! Very pink, evenly coloured sausages may have a low meat content and be bulked up with cereal.

## How to use them:

Sausages need to be cooked slowly over a low heat if you don't want the casings to burst. Pricking them helps drain some of the fat out. They can be grilled, fried, braised or barbecued, and eaten hot or cold.

## What's available?

Sausages come in a multitude of flavours and sizes. Some flavours are traditional, others change as often as fashion.

* Pork sausages are usually flavoured with sage, parsley, garlic or even apple. The small thin ones are chipolatas.

* Beef sausages are darker with a stronger flavour. They often have tomato added.

* Lamb sausages are strongly flavoured, often with the addition of garlic and rosemary, or chilli.

* Chicken sausages look pale and have a very mild flavour. Boudin blanc (white sausages) are often made from chicken.

An old favourite, this salad comes in many versions. Originally it was made with coddled eggs and no bacon, but the addition of bacon turns it into a meal.

# caesar salad

cos lettuce  1

French bread stick  8 thin slices

olive oil  250 ml (1 cup)

bacon rashers  3, rinds cut off, chopped

egg yolk  1

garlic clove  1

anchovy fillets  4

lemon juice  1 tablespoon

Worcestershire sauce  to taste

Parmesan cheese  a lump

serves  2    takes  10 minutes

1 Tear the cos lettuce into pieces and put them in a large bowl. Turn on the grill.

2 Brush the slices of bread on both sides with some of the oil and grill them until they are golden brown all over. Leave to cool.

3 Fry the bacon in a little oil until it browns and then sprinkle it over the bowl of lettuce.

4 Put the egg yolk, garlic and anchovies in a blender and whizz for a minute, then with the motor still running, add the remaining oil in a steady stream through the top hole. The oil and egg should thicken immediately and form mayonnaise. Add the lemon juice and Worcestershire sauce, stir well and season with salt and pepper.

5 Using a potato peeler, make Parmesan curls by running the peeler along one edge of the lump of cheese. Try and make the curls as thin as possible. Make as many curls as you like.

6 Pour the dressing over the lettuce, add the Parmesan curls and toss everything together well. Divide the salad between two bowls and arrange the slices of toasted French bread on each one.

This is a simple salad to throw together at the last minute. Use roasted sesame oil if you can find it because it has a much stronger, fuller flavour. Look for it among the Chinese items in a supermarket.

# bacon and avocado salad

**bacon rashers**  4, rinds cut off

**green beans**  200 g (7 oz) topped, tailed and halved

**baby spinach leaves**  150 g (about 4 handfuls)

**French shallot**  1 finely sliced

**avocado**  1

**brown sugar**  a pinch

**garlic clove**  1 crushed

**olive oil**  2 tablespoons

**balsamic vinegar**  $1/2$ tablespoon

**sesame oil**  1 teaspoon

**serves**  2    **takes**  10 minutes

1 Turn on the grill. Put the bacon on a tray and grill it on both sides until it is nice and crisp. Leave it to cool and then break it into pieces.

2 Bring a saucepan of water to the boil and cook the beans for 4 minutes. Drain them and then hold them under running cold water for a few seconds to cool them down and stop them cooking any further.

3 Put the spinach in a large bowl and add the beans, bacon and shallot. Halve the avocado, then cut it into cubes and add them to the bowl of salad.

4 Mix the brown sugar and garlic in a small bowl. Add the rest of the ingredients and whisk everything together to make a dressing. You can also do this by putting all the dressing ingredients in a screwtop jar, tightening the lid, and shaking the jar for a minute.

5 Pour the dressing over the salad and toss well. Grind some black pepper over the top and sprinkle with some salt.

# spaghetti carbonara

**olive oil**  1 tablespoon

**pancetta**  150 g (5 1/2 oz) cut into small dice

**double (thick) cream**  4 tablespoons

**egg yolks**  3

**spaghetti**  200 g (7 oz)

**Parmesan cheese**  4 tablespoons grated

**serves** 2  **takes** 15 minutes

1 Heat the olive oil in a saucepan and cook the pancetta, stirring frequently, until it is light brown and crisp. Tip the pancetta into a sieve to strain off any excess oil.

2 Mix the cream and egg yolks together in a bowl, and when the pancetta has cooled, add it to the egg mixture.

3 Cook the spaghetti in a large saucepan of boiling salted water until *al dente*, stirring once or twice to make sure the pieces are not stuck together. The cooking time will vary depending on the brand of spaghetti. Check the spaghetti occasionally because packet instructions are often too long by a minute or two. Drain the spaghetti and reserve a small cup of the cooking water.

4 Put the spaghetti back in the saucepan and put it over a low heat. Add the egg mixture and 2 tablespoons of Parmesan, then take the pan off the heat, otherwise the egg will scramble. Season with salt and pepper and mix everything together. If the sauce is too thick and the pasta is stuck together, add a little of the reserved cooking water. The spaghetti should look as if it has a fine coating of egg and cream all over it.

5 Serve the spaghetti in warm bowls with more Parmesan sprinkled over the top.

Spaghetti carbonara is one of the best-known pasta dishes. The sauce is made by cooking egg yolks and cream in the residual heat of the just-cooked pasta. This is enough to cook and thicken the egg without scrambling it.

This variation on a potato cake makes an excellent lunch or supper. For a vegetarian option simply leave out the bacon — it will still be delicious.

# spiced parsnip and bacon cake

**parsnips**  4 cut into pieces

**butter**  3 tablespoons

**bacon rashers**  4, rinds cut off, chopped

**red chilli**  1 finely chopped

**French shallots**  2 finely chopped

**garam masala**  1 teaspoon

**wholegrain mustard**  1 tablespoon

**honey**  1/2 tablespoon

**cream**  3 tablespoons

**serves** 2   **takes** 40 minutes

1 Bring a saucepan of water to the boil and cook the parsnips at a simmer for 15 minutes, or until they feel tender when you prod them with a knife. Drain them well.

2 Melt 2 tablespoons of the butter in a non-stick frying pan, add the bacon and cook it until it starts to brown but is still soft. Add the chilli and chopped shallot and cook for 2 minutes — the shallot should be soft by now. Stir in the garam masala and remove from the heat.

3 Mash the parsnips and mix them into the bacon mixture. Put the frying pan back over the heat with the last tablespoon of butter, pile the parsnip mixture into the pan and flatten it out with a spatula. Cook it for a few minutes — it should brown on the bottom and hold together in a cake. Carefully loosen the cake, slide it out onto a plate, then invert the plate back over the frying pan and flip the cake back in so you can cook the other side.

4 While the cake is cooking, mix the mustard, honey and cream together in a small saucepan over a low heat until the mixture bubbles.

5 When both sides of the cake are brown, turn the cake out onto a board. Cut the cake into wedges and serve with the honey and mustard sauce and some green salad leaves.

Couscous is one of those dishes that sounds difficult but this version, using instant couscous, couldn't be easier. Harissa is a fiery North African spiced chilli paste, which can be bought in tubes or small tins. Merguez are spicy beef or lamb sausages — if you can't find them, you can substitute any other spiced sausages.

# merguez with harissa and couscous

| | |
|---|---|
| butter | 1 tablespoon |
| instant couscous | 150 g (3/4 cup) |
| harissa | 1 teaspoon |
| olive oil | 2 tablespoons |
| lemon juice | 1 tablespoon |
| lemon zest | 1 tablespoon grated |
| parsley | 1 tablespoon chopped |
| chargrilled red capsicum (pepper) sliced | 75 g (2 1/2 oz) |
| raisins | 2 tablespoons |
| merguez sausages | 6 |
| thick natural yoghurt | |

serves 2   takes 30 minutes

1 Put the butter in a saucepan with 250 ml (1 cup) water and bring to the boil. Sprinkle in the couscous, mix it into the water, then take it off the stove. Put a lid on the pan and leave it to sit for 5 minutes. Turn on the grill.

2 Stir the harissa, olive oil, and lemon juice and zest together until well mixed. Add the parsley, red capsicum and raisins and leave everything to marinate briefly.

3 Grill the sausages for 8 minutes, turning them so they brown on all sides.

4 Meanwhile, take the lid off the couscous, stir it for a minute or two to separate the grains, then stir in the harissa mixture.

5 Serve the couscous with the merguez sliced over it and topped with a large dollop of yoghurt.

White beans make a perfect foil for spicy Italian sausages such as salsicce. You can get different varieties of salsicce, so choose one with flavours you like. This recipe can also be made with chorizo sausages.

# salsicce with white beans and gremolata

olive oil  3 tablespoons

salsicce  6 cut into chunks

garlic cloves  4 smashed

chargrilled red or yellow capsicum (pepper)  120 g (4 oz)

tinned cannellini beans  400 g (14 oz) drained and rinsed

lemon zest  1 tablespoon grated

parsley  3 tablespoons chopped

lemon juice  1 tablespoon

extra virgin olive oil  for drizzling

serves 2  takes 30 minutes

1 Heat the olive oil in a frying pan and cook the salsicce until they are browned all over and cooked through. Lift them out of the frying pan with a slotted spoon and put them to one side.

2 Put 2 garlic cloves in the frying pan and cook them over a gentle heat until they are very soft. Cut the capsicum into strips and add them to the pan, along with the beans and salsicce. Stir everything together and cook over a gentle heat for 2 minutes to heat the salsicce through. Season well with salt and pepper.

3 To make the gremolata, smash the remaining two garlic cloves to a paste, with a little salt, in a mortar and pestle. Mix in the lemon zest and the chopped parsley and season with salt and pepper.

4 Just before serving, stir the gremolata through the beans and then finish the dish with a sprinkling of lemon juice and a drizzle of olive oil.

Sausages cooked with lentils is a common dish in France. Toulouse sausages are made from pork. Puy lentils are small, greenish blue and brown lentils, which do not go mushy when cooked. To smash garlic, hit it with the flat side of the blade of a large knife or cleaver and pull off the papery skin.

# braised sausages with puy lentils

olive oil  1 tablespoon

pancetta  55 g (2 oz) cubed

red onion  1 finely chopped

Toulouse sausages  6

garlic clove  1 peeled and smashed

thyme leaves  from 1 sprig

puy lentils  150 g (2/3 cup)

tinned chicken consommé  375 ml (1 1/2 cups)

baby spinach leaves  150 g (about 4 handfuls) finely chopped

crème fraîche  2 tablespoons

serves  2    takes  50 minutes

1 Heat the oil in a wide heavy-based frying pan (one with a lid) and fry the pancetta until it is browned. Take it out, using a slotted spoon, and put it in a bowl. Put the onion in the pan and cook until it is soft and only lightly browned. Take the onion out, using a slotted spoon, and add it to the pancetta. Put the sausages in the same pan and fry them until they are very brown all over. Put the pancetta and onion back in with the sausages.

2 Add the garlic and the thyme leaves to the frying pan, along with the lentils, and mix everything together. Add the consommé and bring everything to the boil. Put a lid on the frying pan and slowly simmer the mixture for 25 minutes. Stir the spinach through.

3 Season the lentils with salt and pepper and stir in the crème fraîche. Serve the sausages with the lentils in shallow bowls. Serve with bread.

# cheese

# Why cheese?

Cheese comes in hundreds of styles and flavours and is extremely well adapted to cooking — nothing on earth melts as well as cheese. Cream cheeses can be used to give a creamy texture to savoury and sweet dishes.

## What to look for:

* If you can, buy loose cheese, cut from a block or in its whole form. If you buy loose cheese, you can often ask to taste it.

* If buying packaged cheese, check the use-by date.

* Avoid pre-grated cheese of any kind as it will never be as good as the stuff you grate yourself.

## How to use it:

* Try to use the type of cheese specified in recipes as different types may not work as well and will change the flavour.

* Choose particular types of cheese for melting: Cheshire, mozzarella, Parmesan, Gruyère, Emmenthal and Fontina melt well. Unripe Brie and Camembert may go stringy, so choose well-ripened ones.

* Grate cheese finely if you are using it in sauces because this will help it melt faster.

# What's available?

* Hard cheeses. These range from Parmigiano Reggiano (Parmesan) and Romano to slightly softer Cheddar, Provolone, Emmenthal and Gruyère.

* Semi-hard cheeses. This category covers cheeses such as Port-Salut, Fontina, haloumi and Edam.

* Soft cheeses. Brie and Camembert have soft, oozing insides and firm (and sometimes furry) white rinds. Pont l'Evêque, Taleggio and Livarot have an orange washed rind and a firmer inside. They range from mild to strong in flavour.

* Unripened cheeses. Fresh cheeses such as cream cheese, cottage cheese, fromage blanc, mascarpone, mozzarella and ricotta are not ripened and have a milky flavour and creamy texture.

* Blue cheeses. These vary from the harder Stilton and Shropshire blue through Gorgonzola and Roquefort to Bleu de Bresse and beautifully creamy torta Dolcelatte. A little of these goes a long way.

* Goat's cheeses. These come as very fresh, soft cheeses such as crottin and chèvre, shaped as pyramids or logs. Matured cheeses are larger and harder.

# goat's cheese, leek and tapenade parcels

**butter**  55 g (2 oz)

**leeks**  2 thinly sliced

**filo pastry**  4 sheets

**tapenade**  1 tablespoon

**thyme sprigs**  2 small

**goat's cheese**  2 small, or 2 thick slices off a log  (100 g/3$^1$/$_2$ oz)

**serves**  2    **takes**  40 minutes

1 Turn the oven on to 180°C (350°F/Gas 4). Melt half of the butter in a saucepan, add the leeks and stir them around to coat them in the butter. Cook them slowly over a low heat until they are completely tender. Leeks take much longer to cook than you think — they will need a good 10 minutes.

2 Melt the rest of the butter in a bowl in the microwave, or in a small saucepan on the stove. Place one of the sheets of filo on the work surface with the short end facing you. Brush the pastry with butter. Lay another sheet right on top of it and cover it with a tea towel to stop the pastry drying out. Do the same with the other two sheets.

3 When the leeks are cooked, uncover the filo. Spread half of the tapenade over the middle of each piece of top pastry, leaving a wide border around the edges. Divide the leeks between the two, putting them on the tapenade. Top each pile of leek with goat's cheese and then a thyme sprig.

4 Now fold the bottom bit of pastry up and the two sides in, to enclose the filling, then fold the top end of the pastry down and roll the whole parcel over. Repeat with the other parcel. Brush the pastry with the rest of the butter and bake the parcels for 20 minutes. The pastry should be browned and crunchy and the filling melted and oozing. Serve with a green salad.

Filo pastry is a useful thing to keep in the freezer. Sheets can be peeled off as you need them and the rest of the packet returned to the freezer. You can use any kind of goat's cheese, depending on how mild you like your cheese.

This recipe makes a lovely, hot, cheesy snack or, if you serve it with salad or roast tomatoes, a comforting supper or lunch. You can vary the types of cheese if you like, but make sure you use something strong enough to complement the mustard.

# cauliflower rarebit

ciabatta  4 thick slices

garlic clove  1

cauliflower  400 g (14 oz) cut into small florets

Gruyère cheese  60 g (1/2 cup) grated

Cheddar cheese  60 g (1/2 cup) grated

Dijon mustard  2 teaspoons

egg  1 beaten

beer  1 tablespoon

cream  2 tablespoons

serves  2    takes  20 minutes

1 Turn on the grill and toast the ciabatta. Cut the garlic clove in half and rub the cut sides over one side of each slice of ciabatta.

2 Bring a saucepan of water to the boil and cook the cauliflower for about 5 minutes, or until it is tender when you prod it with a knife. Drain it very well.

3 Mix the cheeses, mustard, egg, beer and cream together. Put the toast on a baking tray and arrange some cauliflower on top of each piece. Divide the cheese mixture among the pieces of toast, making sure you coat all the cauliflower.

4 Put the rarebits under the grill and grill them until they are brown and bubbling.

Aïoli is a classic, strongly flavoured garlic mayonnaise. The easy version of aïoli in this recipe can also be served with salads, egg dishes and fish, or as an accompaniment to hot or raw vegetables.

# toasted cheese, aïoli and ham

ciabatta or Turkish bread  1/2 a loaf

garlic clove  1 crushed

mayonnaise  3 tablespoons

ham  2–4 slices

semi-dried tomatoes  8 chopped

capers  1 tablespoon chopped

Cheddar cheese  4–6 slices

serves  2    takes  10 minutes

1 Turn on the grill. Cut the bread in half horizontally and then into two equal pieces. Toast all the pieces. To make the aïoli, mix the garlic into the mayonnaise and season it well with salt and pepper.

2 Spread the aïoli over the insides of each sandwich. Put a slice of ham on two of the pieces and then divide the semi-dried tomatoes and capers between them. Top with enough cheese slices to make a good layer and put them on a baking tray.

3 Grill the sandwiches until the cheese melts and starts to bubble and then put the tops back on and press them down firmly.

4 Cut each sandwich in half diagonally and enjoy.

These nachos are based on the type you get at street stalls in Mexico. They are usually made with a fresh white Mexican cheese but feta cheese tastes just as good.

# grilled nachos

nachos  300 g (10 oz) packet

tomatoes  2 chopped

red onion  1 finely chopped

jalapeño chillies  2 thinly sliced

lime juice  1 tablespoon

coriander (cilantro)  2 tablespoons chopped

feta cheese  110 g (3/4 cup) crumbled

serves 2  takes 10 minutes

1 Turn on the grill. Arrange the nachos on two ovenproof plates. (Tin or enamel camping plates work well.)

2 Scatter the tomato, onion and chilli on top of the nachos, then drizzle with the lime juice and season with some salt. Scatter the coriander and feta cheese over the top, making sure the nachos are well covered.

3 Grill the nachos until they start to brown around the edges and the cheese starts to melt. Serve hot but be careful of the plates — they will be very hot too.

Fattoush is a Middle Eastern salad that features crispy pieces of bread tossed with vegetables. Sumac, a red spice with a tart flavour, is traditionally used, but if you can't find any, just squeeze a little bit more lemon juice over the salad instead.

# fattoush with fried haloumi

cucumber  1 small

pitta breads  2

garlic clove  1 crushed

lemon juice  1 tablespoon

olive oil  3 tablespoons

spring onions (scallions)  2 sliced

tomatoes  2 diced

green capsicum (pepper)  1 diced

flat-leaf (Italian) parsley  1 big bunch, chopped

mint  1 tablespoon chopped

oregano  1 tablespoon chopped

sumac  optional

haloumi cheese  500 g (1 lb) cut into 4 slices

serves  2  takes  15 minutes

1 Turn on the grill. Peel the cucumber, cut it into quarters lengthways, then cut each piece into thick slices. Put these in a sieve and sprinkle with a little salt to help drain off any excess liquid, which would make the salad soggy.

2 Split each pitta bread in half and toast them on both sides to make the bread crisp. When the bread is crisp, break it into small pieces.

3 Mix the garlic, lemon juice and 2 tablespoons of the oil to make a dressing. Rinse and drain the cucumber.

4 Put the cucumber, spring onion, tomato, green capsicum and the chopped parsley, mint and oregano in a large bowl. Add the dressing and toss everything together well.

5 Heat the last tablespoon of oil in a non-stick frying pan and fry the haloumi cheese on both sides until it is browned. Scatter the bread over the salad and fold it through.

6 Serve the fattoush with the slices of haloumi on top. Sprinkle with a little sumac if you are using it.

These roast vegetables make you feel virtuous despite the melted Camembert smeared over them. The poached eggs should be just runny enough to coat the vegetables when you break the yolks. Serve with bread for mopping up.

# roast vegetables with poached egg and camembert

**baby onions or French shallots** 6

**olive oil** 4 tablespoons

**asparagus** 1 bundle cut into 4 cm (1¹/2 inch) pieces

**zucchini (courgettes)** 2 thickly sliced

**eggplant (aubergine)** 1 cubed

**garlic cloves** 4

**lemon juice** 1 tablespoon

**eggs** 2

**Camembert cheese** 125 g (4¹/2 oz) cubed

**serves** 2  **takes** 40 minutes

1 Turn the oven on to 200°C (400°F/Gas 6). Peel the baby onions and, if they are particularly big, cut a deep cross into each one, leaving them still attached at the root end. Don't leave any root on, just the barest amount to keep the quarters together.

2 Put the oil in a roasting tin and add the onions, asparagus, zucchini and eggplant, along with the garlic, and toss well. Season with salt and black pepper. Put the tin in the oven and roast the vegetables for 20 minutes. Sprinkle on the lemon juice and roast for another 10 minutes.

3 While everything is still roasting, put a large frying pan full of water over a high heat and bring it to the boil. When the water is bubbling, turn the heat down to a gentle simmer. Crack an egg into a cup and slip the egg gently into the water — it should start to turn opaque almost as soon as it hits the water. Do the same with the other egg, keeping them separate. Don't worry if the eggs spread out in the water. Turn the heat down as low as you can and leave the eggs for 3 minutes.

4 Divide the vegetables between two ovenproof dishes. Put the Camembert on top of the vegetables, dividing it between the dishes. Put the dishes back in the oven for a couple of minutes to start the cheese melting.

5 Top each dish with a poached egg and some black pepper.

# pasta

# Why pasta?

Pasta is a good source of carbohydrate and is very simple to cook. Pasta is an ideal ingredient as it can be made to look and taste impressive very easily.

## What to look for:

It is best to use dried pasta unless you can find good-quality fresh pasta, preferably from a specialist pasta shop.

* Egg pasta is made with eggs and a soft wheat flour called 00, or doppio zero.

* Good-quality dried pasta is made with hard durum wheat flour and water.

* Buckwheat pasta is made with a mixture of wheat flour and buckwheat flour.

* Wholewheat pasta is made with wholewheat flour and is heavier in texture and darker in colour.

## How to cook it:

* Cook pasta in plenty of boiling salted water so it has room to move about in the pan and swell in size.

* Adding oil to the water may stop the pasta sticking together but it may also make the sauce slide off too easily.

* Pasta should be cooked until it is 'al dente'. This means 'to the tooth' — the pasta should not be soggy but retain some 'bite'. Test your pasta as it cooks, as some packet instructions result in a very soft pasta.

* Drain your pasta quickly and serve it while still a little wet to stop it sticking together.

## What's available?

* Tiny pasta shapes like stars and risoni are used in soups but can also be used in salads or served as a side dish with meat and chicken. These are sold dried.

* Long tubular pasta like spaghetti, bavette and capellini are used with simple sauces that will stick. Available mainly dried but sometimes fresh.

* Short pasta shapes like penne (tubes), farfalle (butterflies) and conchiglie (shells) go well with thick chunky sauces that get caught in their shapes. Usually sold dried.

* Sheets of pasta such as lasagne are used to make lasagne and can be rolled up to make cannelloni. Sold fresh and dried.

* Filled pasta like tortellini and ravioli are best eaten with light dressings such as butter or oil so you can taste their fillings. Sold fresh and dried.

# linguine with roasted cherry tomatoes

linguine  200 g (7 oz)

red cherry tomatoes  16

yellow cherry tomatoes  16

olive oil  1 tablespoon

garlic clove  1 crushed

spring onions (scallions)  2 sliced

chives  1 bunch finely chopped

black olives  10

extra virgin olive oil  for drizzling

serves  2    takes  15 minutes

1 Cook the linguine in a large saucepan of boiling salted water until *al dente*, stirring once or twice to make sure the pieces are not stuck together. The cooking time will vary depending on the brand of linguine. Check the pasta occasionally as it cooks because the time given on packet instructions is often too long by a minute or two.

2 Cut all the cherry tomatoes in half. Heat the oil in a saucepan, add the garlic and spring onion and let them sizzle briefly. Tip in the cherry tomatoes and cook them over a high heat until they just start to collapse and give off their juices. Add the chives and olives, season with salt and pepper and toss everything together well.

3 Drain the linguine and put it in a large serving bowl or individual bowls. Pour the cherry tomato mixture on top and grind some black pepper over the top. Drizzle with a little bit more olive oil if you like.

A quick and easy pasta dish with a fresh-tasting tomato sauce. If you can't get cherry tomatoes in both colours, use all red or all yellow. This recipe works equally well with grape or Tom Thumb tomatoes.

Horseradish adds a kick to this creamy sauce and complements the sweetness of the prawns. This sauce also works very well with some flaked cooked salmon or trout fillet.

# farfalle with prawns and lemon horseradish cream

farfalle   200 g (7 oz)

olive oil   1 tablespoon

French shallot   1 sliced

tiger prawns (shrimp)   16 peeled and deveined

lemon juice   1 tablespoon

cream   3 tablespoons

lemon zest   2 teaspoons grated

horseradish cream   1 tablespoon

chervil leaves   1 tablespoon

serves 2   takes 15 minutes

1 Cook the farfalle in a large saucepan of boiling salted water until *al dente*, stirring once or twice to make sure the pieces are not stuck together. The cooking time will vary depending on the brand of pasta. Check the pasta occasionally as it cooks because the time given on packet instructions is often too long by a minute or two.

2 Heat the oil in a frying pan and add the shallot. Cook for a minute, then add the prawns. Cook over a high heat for 2 or 3 minutes, or until the prawns have turned bright pink and are cooked through. Add the lemon juice and toss well. Turn off the heat and leave everything in the pan.

3 Put the cream in a glass bowl and whisk it until it just starts to thicken. Don't make it too thick because when you add the lemon zest and lemony prawns the acid will thicken it further. Fold the lemon zest, horseradish cream and chervil into the cream.

4 Drain the farfalle and tip it into a large bowl. Add the prawns and any lemon juice to the bowl, then add the cream mixture. Fold everything together and season with salt and pepper.

# ham, artichoke and spinach lasagne

butter  1 tablespoon

plain (all-purpose) flour  1 tablespoon

freshly grated nutmeg  a pinch

milk  310 ml (1¼ cups)

bay leaf  1

olive oil  1 tablespoon

garlic clove  1 crushed

baby spinach leaves  125 g (about 3 handfuls)

fresh lasagne sheets  3 large

ham  6 slices

artichoke hearts  4 sliced

Parmesan cheese  2 tablespoons grated

serves  2    takes  1 hour

1 Turn the oven on to 180°C (350°F/Gas 4). Heat the butter in a small saucepan over a low heat. Stir in the flour and nutmeg and cook, stirring continuously, for 1 minute. Take the saucepan off the heat and gradually stir in the milk. Add the bay leaf, put the pan back on the heat and simmer everything, stirring the mixture often so it doesn't go lumpy, until the béchamel sauce is the consistency of thick cream. Keep cooking it for a minute or two to make sure the flour cooks properly — if you don't do this, the sauce will taste of uncooked flour. Season with salt and pepper and discard the bay leaf.

2 Heat the olive oil in a frying pan, add the garlic and let it sizzle for a minute before adding the spinach and stirring it around until it wilts. Cook the lasagne sheets in a large saucepan of boiling, salted water for 3 minutes, then drain well. Trim the lasagne sheets to fit a 15 cm (6 inch) square ovenproof dish.

3 Put a ladleful of the sauce into the bottom of the dish and lay a sheet of lasagne on top. Put three slices of ham, half of the spinach and half of the artichokes on top and drizzle with a little more sauce. Top with another lasagne sheet, then another layer of filling. Place the final lasagne sheet on top and pour the rest of the sauce over it. Scatter the Parmesan over the top.

4 Put the lasagne in the oven and turn the oven down to 170°C (325°F/Gas 3). Cook the lasagne for 30 minutes, then let it sit for 5 minutes before serving it. Serve with some green salad leaves.

This lasagne should have lots of filling and a good layer of béchamel sauce on top. When you cook it, put a baking tray on the bottom shelf of the oven to catch any sauce if the lasagne bubbles over.

Puttanesca is a punchy variation on typical tomato sauces for spaghetti. The olives and capers give it a piquant flavour and the chilli adds heat. Although it is traditionally eaten with spaghetti, you can use pasta of any shape.

# spaghetti puttanesca

**spaghetti**   200 g (7 oz)

**olive oil**   1 tablespoon

**onion**   1/2 finely chopped

**garlic clove**   1 finely sliced

**small red chilli**   1 cored, seeded and sliced

**anchovy fillets**   3 finely chopped

**tinned chopped tomatoes**   200 g (7 oz)

**oregano**   1/2 tablespoon finely chopped

**black olives**   8 halved and pitted

**baby capers**   1 tablespoon

**basil leaves**   a handful

**serves**  2    **takes**  15 minutes

1 Cook the spaghetti in a large saucepan of boiling salted water until *al dente*, stirring once or twice to make sure the pieces are not stuck together. The cooking time will vary depending on the brand of spaghetti. Check the pasta occasionally as it cooks because the time given on packet instructions is often too long by a minute or two.

2 Heat the olive oil in a large saucepan and add the onion, garlic and chilli. Gently fry everything for about 6 minutes, or until the onion is soft. Add the anchovies and cook for another minute. Add the tomato, oregano, olive halves and capers and bring everything to the boil. Reduce the heat, season with salt and pepper, and leave the sauce to simmer for 2 minutes.

3 Drain the spaghetti and add it to the sauce. Toss everything together well so that the pasta is coated in the sauce. Scatter the basil over the top and serve.

# spinach and ricotta ravioli

olive oil  1 tablespoon

red onion  1/2 finely chopped

garlic clove  1 crushed

baby spinach leaves  100 g (about 3 handfuls) coarsely chopped

ricotta  125 g (1/2 cup)

egg yolk  1 beaten

Parmesan cheese  1 tablespoon grated

freshly grated nutmeg

won ton wrappers  24

butter  1 tablespoon

sage leaves  1 tablespoon

serves  2    takes  40 minutes

1 Heat the oil in a frying pan, add the onion and garlic and fry them over a low heat for a few minutes until the onion goes soft and translucent. Add the spinach and stir it around until it wilts. If there is any liquid left in the frying pan, turn up the heat and pull the spinach to one side so the liquid can evaporate.

2 Stir the spinach mixture into the ricotta, along with the egg yolk, Parmesan, some nutmeg and some salt and pepper.

3 Brush a little water around the edge of a won ton wrapper and put a teaspoon of filling in the centre. Fold the wrapper over to make a half moon shape and press the edges firmly together. Put the ravioli on a tea towel laid out on your work surface and repeat with the remaining wrappers.

4 Bring a large saucepan of water to the boil and cook the ravioli for a few minutes. They will float to the surface when they are ready. Scoop them out carefully with a slotted spoon and drain them in a colander. Melt the butter in a small saucepan, add the sage and sizzle for a few minutes until the butter browns slightly. Put the ravioli in bowls and pour the butter and sage over them.

These ravioli are made with won ton wrappers, which can be found in Asian and Chinese food shops and some supermarkets. They come in square or round shapes and can be frozen until you need them.

Minestrone is a brilliant meal in a bowl. Traditionally it is cooked for a couple of hours but this version is much quicker. If you want to make this soup in advance, don't add the pasta until the reheating stage, otherwise it will continue to swell and will go very soft.

# minestrone with pesto

olive oil  1 tablespoon

small onion  1 finely chopped

garlic clove  1 finely chopped

parsley  1 tablespoon finely chopped

pancetta  55 g (2 oz) cubed

celery stalk  1  halved, then sliced

carrot  1 sliced

tomato paste (purée)  1 teaspoon

tinned chopped tomatoes  200 g (7 oz)

chicken or vegetable stock
1 litre (4 cups)

zucchini (courgette)  1 sliced

peas  2 tablespoons

runner beans  6 cut into 2 cm
(3/4 inch) lengths

savoy cabbage  a handful shredded

ditalini  2 tablespoons

tinned borlotti beans  100 g (3$^1$/$_2$ oz)

fresh pesto  2 tablespoons
(page 251)

serves 4   takes 55 minutes

1 Melt the oil in a large saucepan and add the onion, garlic, parsley and pancetta. Cook everything over a very low heat, stirring the mixture once or twice, for about 10 minutes, or until the onion is soft and golden. If your heat won't go very low, keep an eye on everything and stir more often.

2 Add the celery and carrot and cook them for 5 minutes. Stir in the tomato paste and tomato with plenty of pepper. Add the stock and bring slowly to the boil. Cover and leave to simmer for 30 minutes, stirring once or twice.

3 Taste the soup for seasoning, adjust if necessary, then add the zucchini, peas, runner beans, cabbage, ditalini and drained and rinsed borlotti beans. Simmer everything for a couple of minutes until the pasta is *al dente*. Serve with some pesto spooned into the middle of each bowl of minestrone.

# noodles

## Why noodles?

Made with flour and either water or egg, noodles come in a variety of flavours, thicknesses and textures. They can be eaten as a side dish, used in stir-fries, soups and salads, or left as uncut sheets and rolled around fillings.

## What to look for:

* Egg noodles are sold both fresh and dried. Fresh ones can be found in chilled cabinets and should be kept refrigerated because of their raw egg content.

* Wheat noodles are usually sold dried but are sometimes found fresh. Dried ones tend to be a little more robust.

* Rice noodles are sold dried or fresh. Fresh ones should be soft and pliable. If they are kept chilled, they will harden and need to be softened in a steamer or microwave before use.

## What's available?

* Soba noodles are Japanese noodles made with buckwheat flour. They are brown.

* Egg noodles are made with duck or hen eggs and flour, and can be used in soups and stir-fries. Ramen are Japanese egg noodles used in soups.

* Wheat noodles are made from water and flour. They come in various thicknesses. Somen are very fine Japanese wheat noodles whereas udon are fatter noodles often used in soups.

* Glass noodles are made from mung bean starch and are also called cellophane noodles because they are translucent. They are sold dry and are very wiry and tough.

* Rice noodles are white and come in varying thicknesses. Vermicelli are the finest and rice sticks are the thickest. Noodle rolls are sheets of fresh rice noodle.

Char siu, the Chinese-style roast pork used for this recipe, can be bought from restaurants in Chinatown. You will see it hanging in the barbecue windows next to the roast ducks and chickens. Ordinary roast pork will also work for this dish, as will pretty much any cooked meat, or even fish.

# ramen noodle soup with char siu

**thin ramen egg noodles**  150 g dried (4 nests)

**chicken stock**  500 ml (2 cups)

**spring onions (scallions)**  2 shredded

**soy sauce**  2 tablespoons

**char siu**  200 g (5 cm/2 inch long piece)

**small bok choy**  1 roughly chopped

**sesame oil**  for drizzling

**serves**  2    **takes**  10 minutes

1 Cook the noodles in a large saucepan of boiling salted water for about 4 minutes, or until they are just cooked, stirring once or twice to make sure they are not stuck together. The cooking time will vary depending on the brand of noodles.

2 Bring the chicken stock to the boil in a saucepan, then add the spring onion and soy sauce. Taste the stock to see if it has enough flavour and, if not, add a bit more soy sauce — don't overdo it though as the soup's base should be quite mild in flavour. Turn the heat down to a simmer. Cut the char siu into bite-sized shreds or slices (small enough to pick up and eat with chopsticks).

3 Drain the noodles and divide them between two bowls. Add the bok choy to the chicken stock, stir it in, then divide the stock and vegetables between the two bowls. Arrange the char siu on top, then drizzle a little sesame oil onto each — sesame oil has a very strong flavour, so you will only need a couple of drops for each bowl.

Rice noodles have a bland, slippery softness that goes very well with strong flavours. The best ones are bought fresh from Chinese and Asian shops and some supermarkets. They will be hard and brittle when cold, so pour boiling water over them to soften them.

# rice noodles with beef, black beans and capsicums

rump steak   150 g (5$^1$/$_2$ oz)

garlic clove   1 crushed

oyster sauce   1$^1$/$_2$ tablespoons

sugar   1 teaspoon

soy sauce   1 tablespoon

black bean sauce   3 tablespoons

cornflour (cornstarch)   1 teaspoon

sesame oil   $^1$/$_2$ teaspoon

flat rice noodles   600 g (1 lb 5 oz) fresh or 300 g (10$^1$/$_2$ oz) dried

oil   1 tablespoon

red capsicum (pepper)   1 shredded

green capsicum (pepper)   $^1$/$_2$ shredded

coriander (cilantro) leaves   a handful

serves 2   takes 15 minutes

1 Cut the steak across the grain into thin slices and put it in a bowl with the garlic, oyster sauce, sugar, soy sauce, black bean sauce, cornflour and sesame oil. Mix everything together, making sure the slices are all well coated.

2 If you are using dried rice noodles, soak them in boiling water for 10 minutes, or until they are opaque and soft. If your noodles are particularly dry, they may need a little longer. Drain the noodles.

3 Heat the oil in a wok or frying pan and, when it is hot, add the capsicums. Stir-fry the capsicums for a minute or two until they are starting to soften, then add the meat mixture and cook for a minute. Add the noodles and toss everything together well. Keep cooking until the meat is cooked through and everything is hot, then toss in the coriander leaves and stir once before turning off the heat. Serve straight away.

# thai-style chicken with glass noodles

coconut cream  2 tablespoons

fish sauce  1/2 tablespoon

palm sugar  2 teaspoons

chicken breast  1 skinned and cut into shreds

glass noodles  60 g (2 1/4 oz)

lemon grass  1 stem

makrut (kaffir lime) leaves  2

red onion  1/2  finely chopped

coriander (cilantro) leaves  a handful chopped

mint  a handful chopped

red chilli  1 large sliced

green bird's eye chillies  2 finely sliced

roasted peanuts  1 tablespoon chopped

lime  1 cut in halves or quarters

serves 2   takes 20 minutes

1 Mix the coconut cream in a small saucepan or a wok with the fish sauce and palm sugar and bring to the boil, then add the chicken and simmer until the chicken is cooked through. This should only take a minute if you stir it a couple of times. Leave the chicken to cool in the sauce. Soak the noodles in boiling water for a minute or two — they should turn translucent and soft when they are ready. Drain them, then, using a pair of scissors, cut them into shorter lengths.

2 Peel the lemon grass until you reach the first purplish ring, then trim off the root. Make two or three cuts down through the bulb-like root, finely slice across it until it starts to get harder, then throw the hard top piece away. Pull the stems out of the lime leaves by folding the leaves in half, with the shiny side inwards, and pulling down on the stalk. Roll up the leaves tightly, then slice them very finely across.

3 Put all the ingredients, except the lime, in a bowl with the noodles and chicken, with its sauce, and toss everything together. Now squeeze the lime pieces over the dish and toss again. (You can adjust the flavouring at the table, if you like, by putting the lime pieces, white sugar, chopped chillies and fish sauce on the table as condiments.)

Thai food combines flavourings that give it a hot, sweet, sour and salty flavour — often all at once. This salad takes a little time to prepare as it involves a lot of chopping, but is very quick to put together. Glass noodles are also called bean thread noodles or cellophane noodles, depending on the brand.

Rice noodle rolls are a dim sum speciality. You can buy lengths of rice noodle roll in Chinese and Asian shops and some supermarkets. If you buy your rice noodle roll from a refrigerated cabinet, you will have to warm it up before you use it, otherwise it will crack. Do this by briefly steaming or microwaving it.

# steamed rice noodle rolls

**barbecued or roast duck** 350 g
(12 oz) (about half a duck)

**rice noodle rolls** 4

**spring onion (scallion)** 1 finely
shredded

**ginger** 1 thick slice, finely shredded

**coriander (cilantro) leaves** a
handful

**oyster sauce** for drizzling

**chilli sauce**

**serves** 2    **takes** 20 minutes

1 Cut the duck into bite-sized pieces. You may have to strip the flesh off the bones first, depending on how you bought it — leave the skin on but trim off any fatty bits.

2 Gently unroll the rice noodle rolls. If they are a bit stiff, steam or microwave them for a minute or two. If they are in a vacuum-wrapped package, you can also drop the wrapped package in boiling water for 5 minutes.

3 Put a pile of duck (a quarter of the whole amount) at one edge of the narrower end of one roll and arrange some spring onion, ginger and coriander over it. Drizzle with about a teaspoon of oyster sauce and roll the sheet up. Repeat this with the remaining sheets. Put the sheets on a heatproof plate.

4 If you are steaming the noodle rolls, put the plate in a bamboo or metal steamer and set the steamer above a saucepan filled with simmering water. Put the lid on and steam for 5 minutes. If you are using a microwave, cover the rolls with plastic wrap and cook them on high for 3 minutes.

5 Serve the rolls cut into lengths with some more oyster sauce drizzled over them and some chilli sauce on the side.

Laksa is one of the best-known Malaysian/ Singaporean dishes. It comes in a variety of guises and this one has a thin, rich soup base. You can use chicken instead of prawns and egg noodles instead of vermicelli. Buy the best laksa paste available or, failing that, use a red curry paste.

# prawn laksa

oil  1 tablespoon

laksa paste  2 tablespoons

coconut milk  250 ml (1 cup)

chicken stock  250 ml (1 cup)

prawns (shrimp)  8 peeled and deveined

rice vermicelli  125 g (2 bundles)

bean curd puffs  4, cut into 3 pieces

cucumber  5 cm (2 inch) piece cut into shreds

bean sprouts  2 handfuls

Vietnamese mint or mint leaves  a few sprigs

sambal oelek

lime wedges

serves  2    takes  20 minutes

1 Heat the oil in a wok or saucepan and add the laksa paste — depending on the brand, you may need to add a little more or less than the recipe says — you can only find this out by trial and error, so start with a little, make up the soup base and then stir in a bit more if you need to. Cook the paste over a medium heat, stirring it to stop it from sticking, for 2 to 3 minutes.

2 Stir in the coconut milk and chicken stock, bring the mixture to the boil and simmer it for 5 minutes. Add the prawns, bring the mixture back to the boil, then reduce the heat and simmer the prawns for 3 minutes — they will turn pink and opaque when they are ready.

3 Cook the rice vermicelli in boiling water for 3 minutes. Drain it and divide it between two deep serving bowls.

4 Divide the bean curd puffs, cucumber and bean sprouts between the bowls, then ladle in the laksa mixture. Garnish the laksa with a sprig or two of Vietnamese mint and a small amount of sambal oelek (be careful as it is very hot). Serve with lime wedges to squeeze into the laksa.

# rice

## Why rice?

Rice is eaten by over half the world's population as a staple food. Brown rice is higher in fibre and B vitamins than white rice, which loses some of these when the husk is removed. Rice goes with all sorts of main courses and it works equally well with curry and stroganoff.

## How to use it:

Use the type of rice stipulated in the recipe. Long- and short-grained rices are not interchangeable and the dish won't turn out the same if you swap them.

* Long-grained rices are good for eating plain, especially aromatic varieties like basmati from India and jasmine from Thailand.

* Short-grained rices are used for sushi, risottos and rice puddings.

* Sticky, or glutinous, rice can be long- or short-grained. It sticks together slightly when cooked.

## What's available?

* Basmati is a long-grained Indian fragrant rice that goes very well with curries. The grains stay separated when cooked.

* Risotto rice comes in several varieties including arborio, carnaroli and vialone nano, and is a short-grained rice. Risotto rice absorbs lots of liquid but stays firm and keeps its shape.

* Jasmine rice is a long-grained aromatic rice that sticks together lightly when cooked.

* Black rice is the most common Thai variety. It is a long-grained rice and is used for making desserts. It turns purple when cooked.

* Camargue red rice is a short-grained rice with a reddish brown bran. It makes good salads.

* Pudding rice is a short-grained rice sold specifically for making rice puddings.

* Japanese rice is a short-grained rice, also called sushi rice, that sticks together lightly when cooked.

* Brown rice is a rice of varying lengths that has not had its bran removed. It is nuttier in flavour and takes longer to cook.

Originally on the breakfast menu of the British upper classes (who took the idea from an Indian rice dish), kedgeree is now eaten at any time of the day. It is usually made with smoked haddock, but salmon looks much more attractive.

# salmon kedgeree

fish or vegetable stock  500 ml (2 cups)

salmon fillet  200 g or 1 thick 8 cm (3 inch) piece

butter  2 tablespoons

oil  1 tablespoon

onion  1 chopped

madras curry paste  1 teaspoon

long-grain rice  100 g (1/2 cup)

egg  1 hard-boiled and cut into wedges

parsley  2 tablespoons chopped

cream  2 tablespoons

lemon wedges

serves  2   takes  30 minutes

1 Put the fish stock in a frying pan and bring it to the boil. Put the salmon fillet in the stock, put a lid on the frying pan and turn the heat down to a simmer. Cook the salmon for 3 minutes, by which time it should feel firm when pressed and look opaque. Lift it out of the stock and flake it into large pieces by pulling it apart gently with your hands.

2 Melt half of the butter in a frying pan with the oil, add the onion and gently cook it over a low heat until the onion softens and turns translucent. Stir in the curry paste, then add the rice and mix everything together until it is all coated. Add the fish stock, mix it in, then bring the mixture to the boil.

3 Simmer the rice with the lid on over a very low heat for about 8 minutes, then add the salmon and cook, covered, for another 5 minutes, by which time all the liquid should be absorbed. If the rice is too dry and not yet cooked, add a splash of boiling water and keep cooking for a minute or two.

4 Stir in the rest of the butter, the egg, parsley and cream (leave the cream out if you like — the kedgeree just won't be as rich) and serve with the lemon to squeeze over.

Risotto is the perfect dish to cook for someone else, preferably someone you can talk to as you cook. Arborio, carnaroli or vialone nano are all relatively common varieties of risotto rice. You can use any of them for this recipe, but remember that cooking times will vary by up to 5 minutes, depending on the type you choose.

# roast tomato risotto

chicken or vegetable stock   500 ml (2 cups)

saffron threads   a small pinch

dry white wine   125 ml ($1/2$ cup)

butter   1 tablespoon

small onion   1 finely chopped

risotto rice   135 g ($2/3$ cup)

olive oil   1 tablespoon

garlic clove   1 crushed

cherry tomatoes   200 g (about 20)

Parmesan cheese   freshly grated

parsley   2 tablespoons finely chopped

serves   2    takes   25 minutes

1 Heat the stock in a saucepan until it is simmering, then leave it over a low heat. Put the saffron into the wine and leave it to soak.

2 Melt the butter in a large, deep heavy-based frying pan, then gently cook the onion until it is soft, but not browned. Add the rice, turn the heat to low and stir well to coat all the grains of rice in the butter.

3 Add the wine and saffron to the rice, turn the heat up to medium and cook, stirring the rice, until all the liquid has been absorbed. Add the hot stock, a couple of ladles at a time, stirring continuously so that the rice cooks evenly and releases some of its starch. This is what gives risotto a creamy consistency.

4 While the rice is cooking, heat the oil in a saucepan, add the garlic and tomatoes, then fry for 2 to 3 minutes over medium heat until the tomatoes are slightly soft and have burst open. Season well.

5 Once all the stock has been added to the rice, taste the rice to see if it is *al dente*. It is impossible to gauge the exact amount of liquid you will need as every risotto will be a little different. If the rice is not yet cooked and you have run out of stock, use water. Stop cooking the rice as soon as it is soft but still has a little texture or bite in the middle of the grain. Taste the risotto and add seasoning if it needs it. Stir in 2 tablespoons of Parmesan and the parsley. Spoon the tomatoes over the top and scatter more Parmesan on top. Serve straight away.

# butternut and feta risotto

olive oil  2 tablespoons

garlic cloves  6 unpeeled

thyme sprig  1

butternut pumpkin (squash)  half a
small one, peeled and cubed

chicken or vegetable stock
500 ml (2 cups)

butter  1 tablespoon

small onion  1 finely chopped

risotto rice  135 g (2/3 cup)

dry white wine  125 ml (1/2 cup)

parsley  2 tablespoons finely chopped

feta cheese  60 g (a handful) crumbled

Parmesan cheese  freshly grated

serves  2    takes  25 minutes

1 Turn the oven on to 200°C (400°F/Gas 6). Put the olive oil in a roasting tin with the garlic, thyme and butternut pumpkin. Coat everything in the oil and season well. Roast in the oven for about 25 minutes, turning everything over once. Take the garlic out of its papery skin but leave it whole. Throw away the thyme.

2 Heat the stock in a saucepan until it is simmering, then leave it over a low heat. Melt the butter in a large, deep, heavy-based frying pan, then gently cook the onion until it is soft, but not browned. Add the rice, reduce the heat to low and stir well to coat all the grains of rice in the butter.

3 Add the wine to the rice, turn up the heat to medium and cook, stirring the rice, until all the liquid has been absorbed. Add the hot stock, a couple of ladles at a time, stirring continuously so that the rice cooks evenly and releases some of its starch. This is what gives risotto a creamy consistency.

4 Once all the stock is added, taste the rice to see if it is *al dente*. It is impossible to gauge the exact amount of liquid you will need as every risotto will be a little different. If the rice is not yet cooked and you have run out of stock, use water. Stop cooking the rice as soon as it is soft but still has a little texture or bite in the middle of the grain. Taste the risotto and add seasoning if it needs it. Stir in the butternut pumpkin, garlic, parsley and feta, squashing the vegetables slightly as you stir. Serve with grated Parmesan.

Another risotto — this time the sweetness of the roast butternut pumpkin and garlic contrast with the feta cheese.

Risi e bisi, which means rice and peas, is the Venetian version of risotto. It is served in a shallow soup bowl and is rather more sloppy than most other types of risotto. If you can only get frozen peas, add them at the end of cooking so they don't become too soft.

# risi e bisi

chicken or vegetable stock  560 ml (2¹/₄ cups)

butter  1 tablespoon

small onion  1 finely chopped

pancetta  50 g (1³/₄ oz) cut into small cubes

parsley  1 tablespoon finely chopped

peas  150 g (1 cup)

risotto rice  100 g (¹/₂ cup)

Parmesan cheese  freshly grated

serves 2    takes 35 minutes

1 Heat the stock in a saucepan until it is simmering, then leave it over a low heat. Melt the butter in a large, deep heavy-based frying pan, then gently cook the onion and pancetta until the onion is soft, but not browned. Stir in the parsley and peas.

2 Add two ladles of the stock to the frying pan and simmer for 6 to 8 minutes. Add the rice and the remaining stock. Simmer until the rice is *al dente* and most of the stock has been absorbed. Stir in a handful of Parmesan, then season and serve.

The spiced rice (pulao) in this recipe can be eaten with pretty much anything. It goes well with curries and roast meat. Equally, the chicken doesn't have to be served with pulao.

# pulao with fried onions and spiced chicken

chicken stock  500 ml (2 cups)

oil  3 tablespoons

cardamom pods  3

cinnamon stick  5 cm (2 inch) piece

cloves  2

black peppercorns  4

basmati rice  135 g (2/3 cup)

coriander (cilantro) leaves  2 handfuls

onion  1 finely sliced

curry paste  1 teaspoon (any type)

tomato paste (purée)  1/2 tablespoon

yoghurt  1 tablespoon

chicken  200 g (about 2 small) skinless breast fillets, cut into strips

thick natural yoghurt

mango chutney

serves  2    takes  30 minutes

1 Heat the stock in a small saucepan until it is simmering. Heat 1 tablespoon of the oil over a medium heat in a large heavy-based saucepan. Add the cardamom pods, cinnamon stick, cloves and peppercorns and fry for a minute. Reduce the heat to low, add the rice and stir constantly for 1 minute. Add the heated stock and some salt to the rice and quickly bring everything to the boil. Cover the saucepan and simmer the rice over a low heat for 15 minutes. Leave the rice to stand for 10 minutes, then stir in the coriander.

2 Heat a tablespoon of the oil in a frying pan and fry the onion until it is very soft. Increase the heat and keep frying until the onion turns dark brown. Drain the onion on paper towels, then add it to the rice.

3 Mix the curry paste, tomato paste and yoghurt together, then mix the paste thoroughly with the chicken strips.

4 Heat the remaining oil in a frying pan. Cook the chicken for about 4 minutes over a high heat until almost black in patches.

5 Serve the rice with the chicken strips, yoghurt and mango chutney.

This meal is a very good way of using leftover rice (you will need about 1½ to 2 cups). You can add just about anything you like to fried rice — chicken, beef and duck all work well, as do pieces of char siu (Chinese barbecued pork). Serve with soy or chilli sauce if you like.

# special fried rice with prawns

long-grain rice   100 g (½ cup)

eggs   2

spring onion (scallion)   1 chopped

peas   2 tablespoons

oil   1 tablespoon

asparagus spears   6 cut into 3 cm (1¼ inch) lengths

prawns (shrimp)   15 peeled, deveined and halved lengthways

sesame oil   1 teaspoon

serves   2   takes   20 minutes

1 Cook the rice in simmering water for 12 minutes, or until it is cooked, then drain. Lightly beat the eggs in a bowl with the spring onion and a pinch of salt.

2 Cook the peas in simmering water for 3 to 4 minutes for fresh, or 1 minute for frozen. Drain and add to the rice.

3 Heat a wok over a high heat, add the oil and heat until very hot. Add the asparagus and prawns and cook, stirring continuously, until the prawns are pink. Reduce the heat, add the egg and lightly scramble. Before the egg is set too hard, add the rice and peas and increase the heat. Stir to separate the rice grains and break the egg into small bits. Season with salt and stir in sesame oil.

chicken

## Why chicken?

Chicken is a light, mostly white meat that is easy to cook. Available whole or in pieces, chicken goes well with myriad flavours.

## What to look for:

* Try to buy free-range chickens as these will have been less intensively reared and therefore probably have more flavour.

* Corn-fed chickens have a yellow colour but often have the same flavour as ordinary chickens.

* There are also superior quality and organic chickens in some butchers or supermarkets.

## How to use it:

Chicken can be cooked by any method but it is very important to make sure it is thoroughly cooked. This means there must not be any raw blood left in the juices. Check whether chicken is cooked by poking a knife blade into a piece — the juices that run out should be completely clear.

## How to look after it:

* Store chicken on the bottom shelf of the fridge. Make sure it is in a container that will not allow any juices to drip out.

* Defrost frozen chicken thoroughly before use.

## What's available?

* Breast. This white meat can be bought with or without skin, on or off the bone, or as a supreme (with just the small wing bone attached). Each breast has one main piece of meat with a small piece of extra meat called a 'false fillet' attached to the underside. Breast meat takes half the time of other joints to cook. As it tends to be dry, it needs to be basted or cooked quickly to keep it moist.

* Drumsticks. The bottom of the leg, made up of darker meat, usually has the skin on. Good in casseroles and stews or barbecued. Drumsticks make good finger food.

* Thighs. These come bone in or out, and with or without skin. The dark meat has more flavour than breast meat. Good for curries, barbecues, grilling and casseroles.

* Whole chickens. Available in different sizes. Chickens may or may not have a package of giblets inside them — remember to check and take it out.

* Poussin. Whole baby chickens. Serve either one or half per person.

* Spatchcock. A small chicken that has been opened out flat. Good for barbecues or grilling.

# roast chicken with garlic and potatoes

medium chicken  1

butter  1 tablespoon softened

lemon  1 cut in half

onion  1 thickly sliced

small potatoes  6 cut in half

garlic cloves  6 unpeeled

thyme sprigs  4

olive oil  2 tablespoons

chicken stock  250 ml (1 cup)

serves  2    takes  1¹/₂ hours

1 Turn the oven on to 200°C (400°F/Gas 6). Rinse the chicken in cold water. Trim off any excess fat (around the neck opening). Cut off the parson's nose (the triangular piece of flesh where the tail should be). Gently push your hand under the skin on the breast to loosen it (there is a membrane down the middle, so either break through it or go down either side). Once the skin is loose, push the butter under the skin and press down to spread it around.

2 Squeeze half of the lemon over the chicken, then push it into the chicken with a couple of onion slices. Tie the legs together. Put the rest of the onion in a roasting tin and sit the chicken on top. Scatter the potatoes, garlic and thyme around the chicken and drizzle with the olive oil. Season well. Put the chicken in the oven and roast for 1 hour. Check it once or twice to make sure it isn't getting too brown — if it is, cover it loosely with a piece of foil.

3 After an hour, pull one leg of the chicken away from the body. If the juices that run out are clear, the chicken is cooked. If the juices are still pink, keep cooking for another 15 minutes, then check again. Take the chicken out of the tin and put the potatoes back in on their own for 20 minutes. Keep the chicken warm under a piece of foil and a tea towel.

4 Put the chicken on a serving plate and squeeze the remaining lemon half over it. Pile the potatoes and garlic around it. The roasting tin will now contain juices, onion and thyme. Put this on the stovetop over a low heat and add the stock. Bring to the boil, stirring so you scrape up any crusty bits in the tin, then strain into a serving jug.

Roast chicken is an easy meal to make. You turn on the oven, throw in the chicken, then go off and amuse yourself while it cooks — simple! If you serve it with a green salad, the whole meal will be even easier to put together.

This light, refreshing salad is quick and easy to make. If you can't find French shallots, use a quarter of a red onion instead. Serve it with steamed rice if you want a more substantial meal.

# vietnamese chicken salad

**cooked chicken**  1 breast or 2 thighs

**lime juice**  1 tablespoon

**fish sauce**  1 tablespoon

**sugar**  a pinch

**bird's eye chilli**  1 finely chopped

**garlic clove**  1 crushed

**French shallot**  1 finely sliced

**bean sprouts**  a handful

**Chinese cabbage**  a handful shredded

**Vietnamese mint or mint leaves**
2 tablespoons finely chopped

**serves**  2    **takes**  10 minutes

1 Take the flesh off the chicken bones and shred it. Discard the skin and bones.

2 Mix together the lime juice, fish sauce, sugar, chilli, garlic and shallot.

3 Bring a saucepan of water to the boil and throw in the bean sprouts. After 10 seconds, drain them and rinse under cold water to stop them cooking any longer.

4 Mix the bean sprouts with the Chinese cabbage, Vietnamese mint and chicken. Pour the dressing over the salad and toss everything together well.

You can buy nearly all the ingredients for this dish from a deli or in jars from a supermarket. Semi-dried tomatoes are slightly plumper and juicier than sun-dried ones — they are also called mi-cuit or sun-blushed tomatoes.

# grilled chicken with capsicum couscous

**instant couscous** 100 g (1/2 cup)

**olive oil** 1 tablespoon

**onion** 1/2 finely chopped

**zucchini (courgette)** 1 sliced

**chargrilled capsicum (pepper)** a couple of pieces of red or yellow, chopped

**semi-dried (sun-blushed) tomatoes** 6 chopped

**orange zest** 1/2 tablespoon grated

**orange juice** 6 tablespoons

**mint** a handful chopped

**chicken** 4 thighs or 2 breasts, skin on

**butter** 1 tablespoon softened

**serves** 2 **takes** 25 minutes

1 Heat the grill. Bring 250 ml (1 cup) water to the boil in a saucepan, throw in the couscous, then take the pan off the heat and leave it to stand for 10 minutes.

2 Heat the oil in a frying pan and fry the onion and zucchini until lightly browned. Add the capsicum and semi-dried tomatoes, then stir in the couscous. Stir in the orange zest, 2 tablespoons of the orange juice and the mint.

3 Put the chicken in a small shallow baking dish and dot it with the butter. Sprinkle with the remaining orange juice and season well with salt and pepper. Grill the chicken for 8 to 10 minutes, turning it over halfway through. The skin should be browned and crisp.

4 Serve the chicken on the couscous with any juices poured over it.

This chicken is eaten as a snack in Vietnam and is served with a sweet chilli dipping sauce. To make it into a more solid meal, it is served here with steamed rice and cucumber, while the sauce is used as a dressing for both the chicken and the cucumber. You can rub the chicken with the paste ahead of time and cook it at the last minute if you like.

# hot and sweet chicken

rice vinegar  4 tablespoons

caster (superfine) sugar  5 tablespoons

garlic cloves  4 crushed

chilli flakes  a pinch

ground coriander  1/2 teaspoon

ground white pepper  1/2 teaspoon

coriander (cilantro)  a bunch finely chopped, including roots and stems

olive oil  2 tablespoons

lemon juice  1 tablespoon

chicken thighs  4 boneless and skinless, cut in half

fish sauce  1 tablespoon

small cucumber  1 peeled and sliced

serves  2    takes  25 minutes

1 Put the vinegar and 4 tablespoons of sugar in a small saucepan, bring to the boil, then turn down the heat and simmer for a minute. Take the mixture off the heat and add a crushed garlic clove, the chilli flakes and a pinch of salt. Leave the dressing to cool.

2 Heat a small frying pan for a minute, add the ground coriander and white pepper and stir it around for a minute. This will make the spices more fragrant. Add the rest of the garlic, the fresh coriander and a pinch of salt. Add half of the oil and lemon juice and mix to a paste. Rub this all over the chicken pieces.

3 Heat the rest of the oil in a wok, add the chicken and fry it on both sides for 8 minutes, or until it is cooked through. Sprinkle in the rest of the sugar and the fish sauce and cook for another minute or two until any excess liquid has evaporated and the chicken pieces are sticky. Serve the chicken with the sliced cucumber and some rice. Dress with the sauce.

Find the best-quality green curry paste that you can for this dish. If you have access to Thai ingredients, buy small green Thai eggplants, but otherwise use a normal purple one. If you can't find Thai basil, use coriander leaves instead.

# green chicken curry

coconut cream  125 ml (1/2 cup)

green curry paste  2 tablespoons

chicken  4 skinless thighs or 2 breasts, cut into pieces

coconut milk  125 ml (1/2 cup)

2 Thai or 1/4 of a purple eggplant (aubergine),  cut into chunks

palm sugar or brown sugar  1 tablespoon

fish sauce  1 tablespoon

makrut (kaffir lime) leaves  2 torn

Thai basil leaves  a handful

large red chilli  1 sliced

coconut milk or cream  for drizzling

serves 2  takes 20 minutes

1 Put a wok over a low heat, add the coconut cream and let it come to the boil. Stir it for a while until the oil separates out. Don't let it burn.

2 Add the green curry paste, stir for a minute, then add the chicken. Cook the chicken until it turns opaque, then add the coconut milk and eggplant. Cook for a minute or two until the eggplant is tender. Add the sugar, fish sauce, lime leaves and half of the basil, then mix everything together.

3 Garnish with the rest of the basil, the chilli and a drizzle of coconut milk or cream. Serve with rice.

Stuffing cream cheese under the skin of the chicken makes the skin go really crispy when it cooks. You can use any kind of cream cheese with herbs, but Boursin works very well. Serve this with mashed or roasted potatoes.

# roast chicken pieces with herbed cheese

**herbed cream cheese**  4 tablespoons

**lemon zest**  1 teaspoon

**chicken**  2 whole legs (Marylands) or breasts, skin on

**leek**  1 cut into chunks

**parsnip**  1 cut into chunks

**olive oil**  1 teaspoon

**serves**  2    **takes**  50 minutes

1 Put the oven on to 200°C (400°F/Gas 6). Mix the cream cheese with the lemon zest. Loosen the skin from the whole legs or chicken breasts and spread 2 tablespoons of the cream cheese between the skin and flesh on each. Press the skin back down and season it.

2 Bring a saucepan of water to the boil and cook the leek and parsnip for 4 minutes. Drain them well and put them in a baking dish. Drizzle with the oil and season well. Put the chicken on top and put the dish in the oven.

3 Roast for 40 minutes, by which time the skin should be browned and the cream cheese should have mostly melted out to form a sauce over the vegetables. Check that the vegetables are cooked and tender by prodding them with a knife. If they need a little longer, cover the dish with foil and cook for another 5 minutes. Keep the chicken warm under foil in the meantime.

Stir-frying is a very efficient way of cooking. It uses only a small amount of oil and, as everything is cooked very quickly, the food retains both its colour and fresh flavour. Make sure you prepare everything before you start cooking. Keep the heat high and cook quickly.

# stir-fried chicken with ginger and cashews

oil  1 tablespoon

spring onions (scallions)  4 cut into pieces

garlic cloves  2 crushed

ginger  4 cm (1¹/₂ inch) piece finely shredded

chicken breast  1 skinless cut into strips

red capsicum (pepper)  1 cut into strips

snow peas (mangetout)  12

cashews  a handful

soy sauce  1 tablespoon

sesame oil  1 teaspoon

serves 2    takes 10 minutes

1 Heat the oil in a wok until it is smoking — this will only take a few seconds. Add the spring onion, garlic and ginger and stir them around for a few seconds. Next, add the chicken and stir it around until it has all turned white. Add the red capsicum and keep stirring, then throw in the snow peas and cashews and stir-fry for another minute or so.

2 Once the red capsicum has started to soften a little, add the soy sauce and sesame oil, toss everything together and then tip the stir-fry out into a serving dish.

3 Serve with rice or noodles and more soy sauce if you like.

Casseroles are nice, simple dishes that require a minimum of preparation and have a very easy cooking method. They taste equally good if they are prepared a day ahead and then reheated. Use really good-quality olives for this — it doesn't matter whether they are green or black.

# chicken casserole with olives and tomatoes

**olive oil**  1 tablespoon

**small onion**  1 chopped

**garlic clove**  1 crushed

**chicken**  4 pieces, skin on

**tomato paste (purée)**  2 teaspoons

**white wine**  a glass

**sugar**  a pinch

**large ripe tomatoes**  4 chopped

**parsley**  2 tablespoons chopped

**green beans**  12 topped, tailed and halved

**olives**  about 12

**serves** 2        **takes** 50 minutes

1 Heat the oil in a flameproof casserole and fry the onion for a minute or two. Add the garlic and the chicken and fry for as long as it takes to brown the chicken all over.

2 Add the tomato paste and white wine, along with the sugar, and stir everything together. Add the tomato and any juices, the parsley and the beans and bring everything to the boil. Turn down the heat, season well and simmer for 30 minutes.

3 Add the olives and simmer for another 5 minutes. The sauce should be thick by now and the chicken fully cooked. Add more salt and pepper, if necessary. Serve with potatoes, pasta or rice.

# best chicken sandwich ever

**chicken breast fillet**  1 skinless cut in half horizontally

**olive oil**  1 tablespoon

**lemon juice**  1 tablespoon

**ciabatta or Turkish bread**  2 large pieces cut in half horizontally

**garlic clove**  1 cut in half

**mayonnaise**

**avocado**  1/2 sliced

**tomato**  1 sliced

**rocket (arugula)**  a handful of leaves, long stems snapped off

**serves**  2    **takes**  10 minutes

1 Flatten out each piece of chicken by hitting it either with your fist, the flat side of a knife blade or cleaver, or with a meat mallet. Don't break the flesh, just thin it out a bit. Trim off any fat or sinew.

2 Heat the oil in a frying pan, add the chicken pieces and fry them on both sides for a couple of minutes, or until they turn brown and are cooked through (you can check by cutting into the middle of one). Sprinkle with the lemon juice, then take the chicken out of the pan. Add the bread to the pan with the cut side down and cook it for a minute, pressing down on it to flatten it and help soak up any juices.

3 Take the bread out of the pan, rub the cut side of the garlic over the surface, then spread all the pieces with a generous amount of mayonnaise. Put a piece of chicken on two of the pieces, season and then layer with the avocado and tomato, seasoning as you go. Finish with the rocket and the tops of the bread, then serve.

Brilliant for eating anywhere, anytime. A piece of chicken fillet makes a delicious alternative to a burger, and when perked up with garlic, lemon and mayonnaise, this sandwich makes a really tasty meal.

# fish and shellfish

## Why fish?

Sometimes billed as a perfect food
(low in calories, high in protein),
fish often falls into the too-hard
basket when it comes to cooking.
Give it a try though, because fish
is actually very easy to cook,
especially if you grill, roast or
pan-fry it. There are hundreds of
varieties out there — experiment
and find types that you like.

## What to look for:

* Whole fish should be firm, with
  shiny scales (assuming they have
  scales) and bright clear eyes.
  They should smell of the sea.

* Pieces of fish should be firm and
  look fresh. The cut surface should
  be moist and not dry or dull.

## What's available?

* Whole fish are good for barbecuing
  because they can be handled
  without breaking. But bear in
  mind that they may be bony.

* Fillets of fish can be bought with
  the skin on or off. If you want to
  barbecue them, leave the skin on
  so the flesh holds together well.

* Fish steaks are generally cut from
  firm fish and may or may not have
  a central bone and skin. Tuna and
  swordfish are cut from a very
  large fish and so are boneless.
  Cod or salmon steaks are often
  cut across the fish and are
  horseshoe-shaped.

## Why shellfish?

Shellfish have a firm, juicy texture
and a sweet flavour that responds
well to many cooking methods.
When steamed they are delicate in
flavour. When grilled or barbecued
they become almost caramelized.

## What to look for:

* Shellfish (except prawns/shrimp)
  should be bought alive or frozen,
  never dead. They should smell of
  the sea: a fishy smell will mean
  they are old and deteriorating.

* Prawns (shrimp) come in a variety
  of sizes. Tiny ones are best
  bought peeled. Larger ones can be
  cooked with their shells on or off.

* Bivalves such as mussels, clams,
  scallops and oysters must be
  bought live. If you want to take
  them out of their shells, steam
  them briefly to loosen the top
  shell. Scallops are often sold
  out of their shells: you can
  choose whether or not to leave the
  orange roe attached. Bivalves will
  be closed when alive and open as
  they get hot when cooked.

* Crabs and lobsters should be
  bought live or already cooked.
  Lobster tails and crab claws hold
  the most meat.

* Squid and octopus can be bought
  cleaned and ready to use, or still
  whole. Squid comes as cleaned
  tubes and rings and is easiest
  to use like this, rather than
  preparing the squid yourself.

...re many versions of this dish around the ... one of them, gambas al pil pil, is often ... in tapas bars. The addition of onion and tomato makes the dish a bit more substantial. You should use large raw prawns — tiger ones are very good. Serve with bread to soak up all the delicious garlicky oil.

# prawns with garlic and chilli

**olive oil** 4 tablespoons

**garlic cloves** 3 crushed

**red onion** 1/2 finely chopped

**dried chillies** 2 cut in half, seeds removed

**prawns (shrimp)** 16 large, peeled and deveined, tails left on

**tomatoes** 2 finely chopped

**parsley or coriander (cilantro)** a handful chopped

**serves** 2    **takes** 15 minutes

1 Heat the oil in a small frying pan or shallow casserole, preferably one that will look good on the table. Add the garlic, onion and chilli pieces, cook for a few minutes, then add the prawns and cook them for about 4 minutes, by which time they should be pink all over.

2 When the prawns are cooked, add the tomato and cook for a minute or two. Season with salt and stir the herbs through. Take the pan to the table, remembering to put it on a heatproof mat. Eat with bread to mop up the juices.

Try to find large, fat, juicy scallops for this, though having said that, fresh baby ones will be better than poor-quality large ones. If you have the scallop shells, you can serve the scallops and salsa in them.

# scallops with avocado salsa

avocado  1/2

tomato  1

red onion  1/4

red chilli  1 small

coriander (cilantro)  a handful chopped

orange juice  2 tablespoons

scallops  8 large or 12 small shucked

olive oil  1 tablespoon

garlic clove  1 crushed

serves  2    takes  15 minutes

1 Cut the avocado, tomato and red onion into equal-sized small cubes. Chop the chilli as finely as you can. Mix all these together gently and stir the coriander through with 1 tablespoon of the orange juice.

2 Clean the scallops by pulling off the small white lump on the side of each one — a piece of membrane should also peel off. Doing this stops the membrane shrinking around the scallops as they cook.

3 Heat the oil in a frying pan and, when it is really hot, add the scallops and garlic. Cook for a minute, then flip the scallops over and cook the other side. Add the rest of the orange juice to the pan and swirl it around — it should evaporate almost immediately.

4 Serve the scallops on a bed of the avocado salsa.

Trout fillets have a delicate flavour that goes nicely with lemon. Their slightly buttery flesh is well suited to being served on a bed of couscous. You can also use salmon fillets for this recipe.

# grilled trout with lemon butter and couscous

**instant couscous**  100 g (1/2 cup)

**olive oil**  1 tablespoon

**onion**  1/2 finely chopped

**chargrilled capsicum (pepper)** a couple of pieces of red or yellow, chopped

**pine nuts**  a small handful

**lemon juice and zest**  from 1 lemon

**mint**  a handful chopped

**rainbow trout fillets**  2 with the skin removed

**butter**  1 tablespoon softened

**serves**  2   **takes**  25 minutes

1 Heat the grill. Bring 250 ml (1 cup) water to the boil in a saucepan and throw in the couscous. Take the pan off the heat and leave it to stand for 10 minutes.

2 Heat the oil in a frying pan and fry the onion until it is lightly browned. Add the capsicum and pine nuts, then stir in the couscous. Stir through half of the lemon juice and zest, along with the mint.

3 Put the trout fillets on an oiled baking tray. Mix the butter with the rest of the lemon zest and spread it on to the fish. Grill the fish for 6 minutes, or until it is just cooked through. Sprinkle on the rest of the lemon juice and season well.

4 Serve the trout (take it off the tray carefully as it hasn't got any skin to help hold it together) on the couscous with any buttery juices poured over it.

Mussels are often eaten with bread to soak up the juices but, in this case, the glass noodles will do the trick. The easiest way to eat mussels is to use one pair of shells like pincers to pull the mussels out of the other shells.

# thai-style mussels

mussels  1 kg (about 1 bag)

glass noodles  120 g (2 small bundles)

garlic clove  1 crushed

spring onion (scallion)  1 finely chopped

red curry paste  1 tablespoon

coconut cream  4 tablespoons

lime juice  from 1 lime

fish sauce  1 tablespoon

coriander (cilantro) leaves  a handful

serves  2    takes  25 minutes

1 Rinse the mussels in cold water and pull off any beards. Now look at each one individually and, if it isn't tightly closed, tap it on the work surface to see if it will close. Throw away any mussels that won't close or are broken.

2 Soak the noodles in boiling water for a minute or two — they should turn translucent and soft when they are ready. Drain them and, using a pair of scissors, make cuts through the noodles to cut them into shorter lengths.

3 Put the mussels in a deep frying pan or wok with the garlic and spring onion and 60 ml (1/4 cup) water. Bring the water to the boil, then put a lid on and cook the mussels for 2 to 3 minutes, or until they are all open. Throw away any that don't open. Tip the whole lot, including any liquid, into a sieve lined with a piece of muslin (a J-cloth or Chux will do), reserving the liquid.

4 Pour the cooking liquid back into the pan, add the curry paste and coconut cream and stir everything together. Bring the mixture to the boil, then add the lime juice and fish sauce. Put the mussels back in the pan. Cook everything for a minute, then stir in the coriander leaves.

5 Put some noodles in each bowl and ladle mussels on top.

Salade Niçoise is usually made with tinned tuna, but this recipe uses fresh tuna steak. Of course, if you don't have fresh tuna, you can use good-quality tinned tuna or even fresh salmon.

# salade niçoise

**salad potatoes**  4 small (300 g)

**small green beans**  12 topped, tailed and halved

**olive oil**  4 tablespoons

**tuna steak**  200 g (7 oz) cubed

**garlic clove**  1 crushed

**Dijon mustard**  1/2 teaspoon

**white wine vinegar**  1 tablespoon

**green lettuce leaves**  a couple of handfuls

**cherry tomatoes**  6 halved

**black olives**  8

**capers**  1 tablespoon drained

**hard-boiled eggs**  2 cut into wedges

**anchovies**  4 halved

**lemon wedges**

**serves** 2   **takes** 25 minutes

1 Cook the potatoes in boiling salted water for about 10 minutes, or until they are just tender. Drain them, cut them into wedges, then put them in a bowl. Cook the beans in boiling salted water for 3 minutes, then drain and hold under cold running water for a minute (this will stop them cooking any further). Add them to the potatoes.

2 Heat a tablespoon of olive oil in a frying pan and, when it is hot, cook the tuna cubes for about 3 minutes, or until they are browned on all sides. Add these cubes to the potatoes and beans.

3 Whisk together the garlic, mustard and vinegar, then add the remaining oil in a thin, steady stream, whisking until smooth. Season well. You can also do this by putting all the dressing ingredients in a screwtop jar (with the lid on) and shaking it for a minute.

4 Cover the base of a large bowl with the lettuce leaves. Scatter the potatoes, beans, tuna, tomatoes, olives and capers over the leaves, and drizzle with the dressing. Decorate with the egg wedges and anchovies. Squeeze some lemon juice over the salad.

Fish cakes are one of the most divine comfort foods. You can use any type of firm, white fish you like — cod, haddock and ocean perch work well.

# saffron fish cakes with herb crème fraîche

milk  80 ml (1/3 cup)

saffron threads  a pinch

white fish fillets  250 g
(about 2 medium fillets)

large potatoes  2 cut into chunks

garlic clove  1 unpeeled

plain (all-purpose) flour  1
tablespoon

lemon zest  2 teaspoons grated

parsley  a handful finely chopped

cream  1 tablespoon

crème fraîche  4 tablespoons

mint  1 tablespoon finely chopped

parsley  1 tablespoon finely chopped

butter  1 tablespoon


serves  2    takes  35 minutes

1 Put the milk and saffron in a frying pan and heat until simmering. Add the fish, turn up the heat a little and cook until the fish turns opaque and flaky — you might need to turn it over halfway through. Don't worry if it breaks up. Lift the fish out of the milk into a bowl and break it up roughly with a fork. Keep the milk.

2 Cook the potato and garlic clove in simmering water for about 12 minutes, or until the potato is tender. Drain the potato and put it back in the saucepan. Peel the garlic and add it to the potato, mash everything together and strain in the saffron milk. Keep mashing until the mixture is smooth, then stir in the fish, flour, 1 teaspoon of the lemon zest, the parsley and cream. Season well.

3 Make the mixture into four even-sized cakes. Don't squeeze them too much — they don't need to be perfect — a rougher, looser texture will taste and cook better. Put them in the fridge to chill while you make the herb crème fraîche.

4 Mix together the crème fraîche, remaining lemon zest and herbs. Heat the butter in a non-stick frying pan and cook the fish cakes for 3 minutes on each side — they should have a nice brown crust and heat all the way through. Serve with the crème fraîche.

# salmon nori roll with sesame noodles

**soba noodles**  150 g (about half a packet)

**sesame oil**  1 teaspoon

**sesame seeds**  1 tablespoon

**salmon fillet**  10 x 15 cm (4 x 6 inch) piece, bones removed

**nori**  1 sheet

**butter**  1 tablespoon

**baby spinach leaves**  120 g (about 4 handfuls)

**serves** 2   **takes** 30 minutes

1 Cook the noodles in a large saucepan of boiling salted water for about 5 minutes, or until they are just cooked, stirring once or twice to make sure they are not stuck together. The cooking time will vary depending on the brand of noodles. Drain the noodles, add the sesame oil and some seasoning, then toss them so they are coated in the oil. Dry-fry the sesame seeds in a frying pan until they start to colour and smell toasted, then add them to the noodles. Cover and keep warm.

2 Cut the salmon fillet in half horizontally and neaten the edges. Cut the sheet of nori in half with a pair of scissors and lay a piece of salmon fillet on top of each half. Season well, then roll up the fillets to make neat log shapes. Trim off any bits of nori or salmon that stick out. Using a sharp knife, cut each roll into three pieces.

3 Heat the butter in a non-stick frying pan and fry the pieces of roll until they are golden on each side and almost cooked all the way through. This will probably take about 4 minutes on each side. Lift out the salmon. Add the spinach to the pan, stir it around until it wilts, then turn off the heat.

4 Serve the salmon with the noodles and some spinach on the side.

You must cook these nori rolls quite soon after making them up or the nori will start to go a bit soggy. The rolls taste good with mashed or crushed potatoes if you don't want noodles.

Oysters don't have to be eaten raw — they cook well and are delicious steamed with a few flavourings. If your oysters are closed, steaming them for a minute will make them much easier to open than toiling with an oyster knife.

# steamed oysters with ginger and soy

oysters   12 shucked or unshucked

ginger   1 cm (1/2 inch) piece finely shredded

spring onion (scallion)   1 finely shredded

red chilli   1/2 finely shredded

light soy sauce   3 teaspoons

sesame oil

serves  2    takes  10 minutes

1 Put your oysters on two plates, which you have covered with a layer of rock salt if possible — this will stop them tipping over and spilling their juices. Put each plate in a steamer basket and put the steamers over a saucepan of simmering water. Put the lid on and wait for a minute. If your oysters still have their shells you should be able to lift them off by now.

2 Sprinkle some ginger, spring onion and chilli on each oyster and add a quarter of a teaspoon of soy sauce and a drop of sesame oil to each. Cook for another minute with the lid on — the oysters will look slightly opaque when they are ready.

3 Serve the oysters on their bed of rock salt.

This is an easy version of a curry from Goa in South India. You can use just about any curry paste, but a vindaloo one would be best as it originates from Goa. The sauce should be quite thick so that you can scoop it up with pieces of Indian bread.

# goan prawn curry

oil  1 tablespoon

curry paste  1 tablespoon

onion  1/2 finely chopped

tomato  1 chopped

garlic cloves  2 chopped

green chilli  1 finely chopped

ginger  1 cm (1/2 inch) piece grated

tamarind purée  1 tablespoon

coconut cream  2 tablespoons

prawns (shrimp)  10 peeled and deveined

serves 2   takes 25 minutes

1 Heat the oil in a deep frying pan and fry the curry paste for about a minute, by which time it should start to be aromatic. Add the onion and fry until it is golden. Add the tomato, garlic, green chilli and ginger and fry over a low heat, stirring occasionally, for about 10 minutes, or until the oil separates out from the sauce.

2 Add the tamarind to the pan and bring everything to the boil. Add the coconut cream and stir. Season with salt.

3 Add the prawns and bring everything slowly to the boil. (The sauce is not very liquid, but it needs to be made very hot in order to cook the prawns.) Simmer the prawns for 3 minutes, or until they turn bright pink all over. Stir them around as they cook. Serve with rice or Indian breads.

pork

## Why pork?

Pork, often referred to as 'the other white meat', contains more iron, thiamine, riboflavin and zinc than chicken or fish. It is lower in kilojoules and fats than red meats and can be cooked in the same way. For pork that has a lower fat content, buy trimmed cuts or trim off all visible fat yourself.

## What to look for:

Pork should have firm white fat and pale pink flesh. Avoid any pork that looks wet and floppy or has waxy, yellow fat. Organic pork will generally be of a better quality and flavour than intensively farmed pork because what the animal is fed affects the flavour of the meat. Look out for pork from special breeds of pig at your butcher shop.

## How to look after it:

* Unwrap any packaging as soon as you get home, wipe the meat dry, put it on a clean plate and cover with plastic wrap. Put it in the fridge on a lower shelf.

## What's available?

* Pork chops. These come from different parts of the pig such as the loin and ribs. Chops are good for grilling, pan-frying and barbecuing.

* Pork ribs. Buy either meatier American-style spareribs, or the Chinese ones, which are bonier but barbecue and braise well. Ribs are best cooked by simmering them in water until tender and then cooking them in a sauce.

* Minced pork. This is paler than minced beef or lamb and can be quite moist and fatty. It is good for making meatballs and meatloaf.

* Legs of pork. These are best cooked slowly as they don't have much fat. Legs are good for roasts.

* Loin of pork. Can be bought on or off the bone. Boned loin is often sold rolled up as a joint. Loin is also sold cut into chops, or off the bone and cut into cubes.

* Pork fillet. The easiest cut to cook and quite delicate in flavour. Sold whole or cut into medallions.

* Ham. This is wet- or dry-cured pork and is sold smoked or unsmoked. Ham has a stronger, richer flavour than pork that hasn't been cured, and is often quite sweet.

Found in almost every Chinese restaurant and tainted with the stigma of naffness, this is one of the yummiest dishes. To add a piquant flavour, buy a jar of Chinese pickles and add a tablespoon to the sauce.

# sweet-and-sour pork

pork loin  300 g (10 oz) cubed

egg  1

cornflour (cornstarch)  3 tablespoons

oil  3 tablespoons

onion  1/2 cubed

red capsicum (pepper)  1/2 cubed

spring onion (scallion)  1 cut into lengths

clear rice vinegar or white vinegar  125 ml (1/2 cup)

tomato ketchup  2 tablespoons

sugar  110 g (1/2 cup)

serves  2   takes  30 minutes

1 Put the pork cubes and egg in a bowl with 2 tablespoons of the cornflour. Stir everything around to coat the pork well, then tip everything into a sieve and shake off any excess cornflour.

2 Heat a wok over a high heat, add a tablespoon of oil and heat it until it just starts to smoke. Add the onion and cook it for a minute. Add the red capsicum and spring onion and cook for another minute. Add the rice vinegar, tomato ketchup and sugar, turn down the heat and stir everything together until the sugar dissolves (if the sugar has not dissolved, the mixture will feel gritty as you stir). Bring to the boil and simmer it for about 3 minutes.

3 Mix a tablespoon of cornflour with a tablespoon of water, add it to the sweet-and-sour mixture, then simmer for a minute until the sauce thickens a bit. Pour the sauce into a bowl.

4 Heat the remaining oil in a non-stick frying pan over a medium heat. As soon as the oil is hot, slide the pork cubes into the pan and cook them until they are browned and crisp. Add the sauce and reheat everything until the sauce is bubbling.

This recipe is based on a French one from Normandy. If you happen to have any Calvados in your drinks cupboard, you can add a shot of it, along with the cider, for a stronger flavour. Snipping the fat on the pork chops will stop them curling up as they cook.

# pork chops with apples and cider

oil  1 tablespoon

onion  1 sliced

Golden Delicious apple  1 cored and cut into wedges

caster (superfine) sugar  1 teaspoon

butter  1 teaspoon

pork chops  2 thick, snipped around the edges

cider  2 tablespoons

cream  2 tablespoons

serves 2  takes 25 minutes

1 Heat the oil in a non-stick frying pan, add the onion and fry for about 5 minutes, or until soft and just beginning to brown. Tip the onion out onto a plate.

2 Add the apple wedges to the pan and fry them for a minute or two — they should not break up, but should start to soften and brown. Add the sugar and butter and shake everything around in the pan until the apples start to caramelize. Add the apples to the onion.

3 Put the pork chops in the frying pan, add a bit of seasoning and fry them for 4 minutes on each side, or until they are cooked through. Put the onion and apple back in the pan and heat them up, then add the cider and bring to a simmer. Once the liquid is bubbling, add the cream and shake the pan so everything mixes together. Let it bubble for a minute, then season well and serve with potatoes and a green salad — watercress goes particularly well.

# roast pork with crackling

**joint of pork on the bone**  about 1.5 kg (3 lb)

**thyme sprigs**  3

**garlic cloves**  6

**baby onions**  8

**potatoes**  6 cut into quarters

**olive oil**  2 tablespoons

**Granny Smith apples**  3 peeled and chopped

**caster (superfine) sugar**  1/2 tablespoon

**butter**  1 teaspoon

**plain (all-purpose) flour**  1 tablespoon

**chicken stock**  250 ml (1 cup)

**serves**  6    **takes**  2 hours

1 Turn the oven on to 200°C (400°F/Gas 6). Put the joint of pork on a chopping board and remove the layer of skin in one piece by peeling it off — you might need to help it along a bit with a knife blade. Trim off all but a thin layer of fat from the joint — don't trim it all off or your joint will be horribly dry when you eat it. Score lines into the skin using a very sharp kitchen knife or a Stanley knife from your tool box, then rub some salt into the skin. Put the skin back on top of the joint, tucking the thyme between the skin and fat.

2 Put the joint with the bone side down in a roasting tin, along with the garlic, onions and potatoes. Drizzle the vegetables with the oil and make sure all the potatoes are coated. Cook the joint for 1 hour 20 minutes, then check whether it is cooked. Do this by pushing a skewer into the meat, leaving it for 5 seconds, then pulling it out and feeling how hot it is. If it is very hot, the meat will be cooked. If not, continue cooking and check every 10 minutes.

3 While the meat is cooking, cook the apple with the sugar and butter and a tablespoon of water until they turn into a purée. Mash them with the back of a spoon if necessary.

4 When the meat is cooked, take it out and leave it to rest for 10 minutes. Take the potatoes, garlic and onions out of the tin. Spoon off the fat and put the tin over a low heat. Add the flour and stir it in. Cook the flour, stirring constantly for a minute, then add the stock and let it bubble for a minute until it thickens — this will make a thin gravy from the meat juices.

5 Loosen the chine bone from the joint by running the point of a knife around it. Carve off meat slices, leaving rib bones attached to some and cutting between the bones for others.

In order to make a good roast pork with crackling, you will need a reasonably large piece of meat — so invite some friends to share this with you. Make sure you buy a joint that is easy to carve. Cook some easy vegetables such as carrots or broccoli to go with it.

Pickled eggplant is a good accompaniment to this pork dish but can be omitted if you prefer. Make sure you cook the meat on a medium heat so the marinade doesn't burn. You can also cook pork chops or chicken pieces in the same way.

# pork loin with pickled eggplant

pork loin fillet  a 500 g (1 lb) piece
(about 10 cm/4 inches long)

hoisin sauce  1 tablespoon

five-spice powder  a pinch

oil  3 tablespoons

eggplant (aubergine)  1/2 cut into
wedges

soy sauce  1 tablespoon

sesame oil  1 teaspoon

balsamic vinegar  1 tablespoon

caster (superfine) sugar  a pinch

bok choy  1 cut into quarters

serves 2   takes 20 minutes

1 Put the pork in a dish and add the hoisin sauce, five-spice powder and a tablespoon of oil. Rub the mixture over the pork and set it to one side.

2 Heat another tablespoon of oil in a non-stick frying pan and add the eggplant. Fry it until it softens and starts to brown, then add the soy sauce, sesame oil, vinegar and sugar and toss everything together for a minute. Tip the eggplant out onto a plate and wipe out the frying pan.

3 Put the last tablespoon of oil in the frying pan and put it over a medium heat. Add the pork and fry it on all sides until it is browned and cooked through. The time this takes will depend on how thick your piece of pork is — when it is cooked, it will feel firm when pressed. Put the eggplant back in the pan to heat through.

4 Take out the pork and leave it to sit for a minute or two. Cook the bok choy in a saucepan with a little bit of boiling water for 1 minute, then drain well. Slice the pork into medallions and serve it with the pickled eggplant and bok choy.

Witlof, or chicory, has a pleasantly bitter flavour that goes well with the sweetness of the ham. Choose chicory that is still yellow — it is often sold wrapped in paper to prevent it from going green. The greener it is, the more bitter it will be. Red witlof are sometimes available.

# ham braised with witlof

oil  1 tablespoon

butter  1 teaspoon

witlof (chicory/Belgian endive) heads  2 sliced horizontally

leg ham  4 thick slices

brown sugar  2 teaspoons

white wine  1/2 glass

parsley  1 tablespoon chopped

serves 2   takes 20 minutes

1 Heat the oil in a large frying pan, add the butter and when it is sizzling, add the witlof, with the cut side down, and fry it for a minute. Add the slices of ham to the pan and fry them briefly on each side. Add the sugar and wine to the pan, season well and cover it with a lid. Cook for about 3 minutes, or until the witlof is soft.

2 Take the lid off the pan, turn the heat up and let the sauce bubble until it has thickened and gone quite sticky. Stir in the parsley.

# lamb

## Why lamb?

Lamb is a tender meat whether you cook it quickly or slowly. It can be cooked in many different ways, goes well with both herbs and spices, and always tastes good.

## What to look for:

Lamb should look dry and freshly cut, with pink flesh and fat that looks white, firm and waxy, not yellow and oily. For less fatty meat, choose cutlets, which you can trim, or pieces of loin, as these are naturally less fatty.

## How to look after it:

* Unwrap any packaging as soon as you get home, wipe the meat dry, put it on a clean plate and cover with plastic wrap. Put it in the fridge on a lower shelf.

* If you are not using the lamb the same day, brush both sides of the meat with olive oil to stop it going brown (oxidizing).

## How to serve it:

Always serve lamb on a hot plate so the fat doesn't congeal too quickly.

## What's available?

* Best end of neck, or rack of lamb, has six or seven chops or cutlets. These can be separated into individual cutlets or cooked as a rack. Cutlets with the bones cleaned are 'French-trimmed' cutlets. Cutlets cook quickly and are good for barbecuing, grilling or frying.

* Noisettes are made by boning cutlets and chops from the best end and loin, and tying the meat into neat rounds. They are quick to cook and look very attractive.

* Leg of lamb is a good joint for roasting. It can be bought on and off the bone.

* Eye of loin, or lamb fillet, is a long, lean piece of meat, which is very tender. It is good for pan-frying and grilling.

* Lamb backstraps are lengths of meat cut from beside the backbone. Fillet and loin of lamb are sometimes labelled backstrap.

Lamb shanks don't need much preparation before you put everything in a casserole over a low heat and leave it to cook. Harissa is a hot sauce made from chillies and spices, available in jars and tubes. If you can find preserved lemon, use it, otherwise use lemon zest. Serve the dish with couscous or rice.

# lamb shanks with chickpeas

oil  1 tablespoon

lamb shanks  2 large or 4 small

onion  1 finely chopped

garlic clove  1 crushed

harissa  2 teaspoons

cinnamon stick  1

tinned chopped tomatoes  400 g (14 oz)

tinned chickpeas  300 g (10¹/₂ oz)
drained

green olives  8

preserved lemon or lemon zest
¹/₂ tablespoon finely chopped

mint  1 tablespoon chopped

serves 2    takes 1¹/₂ hours

1 Heat the oil in a casserole over a medium heat and fry the lamb shanks until they are well browned all over. Add the onion and garlic and fry them for a couple of minutes until the onion starts to soften.

2 Add the harissa, cinnamon and salt and pepper to the casserole, stir everything together, then add the chopped tomato and bring everything to the boil. If there doesn't seem to be enough liquid (the shanks need to be pretty well covered), add a bit of water. Put the lid on and turn the heat down until the liquid is simmering, then cook for 40 minutes.

3 Add the chickpeas, olives and lemon to the pan and stir them into the liquid. Season to taste and continue cooking with the lid off for another 15 to 20 minutes. By this time, the lamb should be very tender and almost falling off the bone. If it isn't, just keep cooking it, checking every 5 minutes until it is. Using a big spoon, scoop any orange-coloured oil off the top, then stir in the mint. Serve with extra harissa if you would like the sauce a little hotter.

You can use lamb chops or slices of lamb loin for this recipe if you prefer. Make sure that you cook the onion marmalade long enough for the onions to go meltingly soft and sweet. If you undercook it the onions will be acidic. This recipe goes very well with mash.

# lamb cutlets with onion marmalade

| | |
|---|---|
| butter | 1 tablespoon |
| olive oil | 2 tablespoons |
| onions | 2 finely sliced |
| brown sugar | 1 teaspoon |
| thyme leaves | 1 teaspoon |
| parsley | 1 tablespoon finely chopped |
| lamb cutlets | 6 French-trimmed |
| lemon juice | 1 tablespoon |

serves 2    takes 30 minutes

1 Heat the butter and 1 tablespoon of the olive oil together in a saucepan. Add the onion, sugar and thyme and stir well. Turn the heat to low, cover the saucepan and cook the onion, stirring it occasionally for 20 to 25 minutes, or until it is very soft and golden. Season well, stir the parsley through and keep it warm over a very low heat.

2 Heat the remaining oil in a frying pan or brush a griddle with oil and, when it is hot, add the cutlets in a single layer. Fry for 2 minutes on each side, or until the lamb is browned on the outside but still feels springy when you press it. Add the lemon juice and season well.

3 Put a small pile of the onion marmalade on each plate and place the cutlets around it.

# herbed rack of lamb with orange sweet potato mash

**parsley**  1 tablespoon finely chopped

**thyme**  1 teaspoon finely chopped

**lemon zest**  1 teaspoon grated

**Dijon mustard**  1 tablespoon

**lamb**  1 x 6-cutlet rack, French-trimmed and excess fat removed

**olive oil**  1 tablespoon

**orange sweet potato**  600 g (1¼ lb) (about 2) peeled and cubed

**butter**  1 tablespoon

**ground cumin**  ½ teaspoon

**serves**  2    **takes**  35 minutes

1 Turn the oven on to 220°C (425°F/Gas 7). Put the herbs and lemon zest in a small bowl with the mustard, add plenty of salt and pepper and mix well. Firmly press the herb mixture onto the outside, skinned side of the rack. Leave the sides and bone side of the rack clean. Put the rack, with the herbed side up, in a roasting tin.

2 Drizzle the olive oil over the lamb and put it in the oven on the top shelf. Roast the lamb for 20 minutes if you like your lamb rare. If you would like it cooked to medium, cook it for another 5 minutes, and if you would like your lamb cooked right through, give it another 10 minutes. By now, the herb crust should be browned. When the lamb is cooked, take it out of the oven, cover it with a piece of foil and leave it to rest for 5 minutes — this allows the juices to soak back into the meat.

3 To make the mash, put the orange sweet potato in a large saucepan of water and bring it to the boil. Turn the heat down and cook at a simmer for 10 minutes, or until the sweet potato is tender. Test it by pushing the point of a knife into a piece — if it slips easily off the knife, it is ready. Drain. Put the saucepan back on the heat and add the butter and cumin. Let the cumin sizzle for a minute, then add the sweet potato and remove the saucepan from the heat again. Use a potato masher to mash the sweet potato until it is smooth. Season it well with salt and pepper.

4 Carve the lamb into separate cutlets by cutting between the bones. Put a pile of orange sweet potato mash on each plate and top it with the cutlets.

Herbed rack of lamb is delicious with orange sweet potato mash but you can serve it with any type of potatoes. Make the mash while the lamb is cooking and then they should both be ready at roughly the same time.

Ready-made curry pastes work very well when you are short of time or don't have the right combination of spices in the cupboard. Pastes vary in strength, so you may need to adjust the amount you use. If you need to bump up the heat, you can stir in some more halfway through, so taste the sauce as soon as you have added the last bit of yoghurt.

# lamb curry

lamb   500 g (1 lb) leg or shoulder cubed

thick natural yoghurt   2 tablespoons

onion   1 chopped

green chilli   1 roughly chopped

garlic clove   1 crushed

ginger   1 cm (1/2 inch) piece grated

cashew nuts   2 tablespoons

korma curry paste   2 tablespoons

oil   2 tablespoons

serves  2    takes  2³/₄ hours

1 Put the lamb in a bowl with 1 tablespoon of the yoghurt and mix together until all the meat cubes are coated.

2 Put the onion with the chilli, garlic, ginger, cashew nuts and curry paste in a blender, add 2 tablespoons of water and process to a smooth paste. If you don't have a blender, finely chop everything before adding the water.

3 Heat the oil in a casserole over a medium heat. Add the blended mixture, season it with salt and cook it over a low heat for 1 minute, or until the liquid evaporates and the sauce thickens. Add the lamb and slowly bring everything to the boil. Cover the casserole tightly, simmer for 1 hour, then add the rest of the yoghurt and keep cooking for another 30 minutes, or until the meat is very tender. Stir the meat occasionally to prevent it from sticking to the pan. The sauce should be quite thick. Serve with rice.

You can eat these as a snack, starter or as part of a meal. If you want to serve them as finger food, scrape the bone ends clean with a knife blade so they are easy to pick up. You can vary the heat by using more or less Tabasco.

# spiced lamb cutlets

**Tabasco sauce**  a few drops

**ground turmeric**  $1/2$ teaspoon

**garam masala**  $1/4$ teaspoon

**garlic clove**  1 crushed

**thick natural yoghurt**  1 tablespoon

**lemon juice**

**lamb cutlets**  8, fat trimmed off

**serves**  2  **takes**  10 minutes plus marinating

1 Mix together the Tabasco, turmeric, garam masala, garlic and yoghurt to form a paste, adding a few drops of lemon juice. Rub the paste over the cutlets, then put them on a plate, cover them and put them in the fridge for about 2 hours. This will allow the flavours to mix and the yoghurt to tenderize the meat.

2 Turn the grill to its highest setting. Sprinkle the chops with salt on both sides, put them on a wire rack and grill them for 2 to 3 minutes on each side, or until they are browned and sizzling. Squeeze a little more lemon juice over them when they are cooked.

Real comfort food, shepherd's pie is easy to make and easy to eat. You can use leftover cooked lamb from a roast, or lamb mince — they work equally well. Serve with peas or another green vegetable.

# shepherd's pie

oil  1 tablespoon

onion  1/2 finely chopped

carrot  1/2 finely chopped

minced (ground) lamb  500 g (1 lb) raw or cooked

plain (all-purpose) flour

tomato ketchup  1 tablespoon

beef stock cube  1

Worcestershire sauce

potatoes  3 cut into chunks

milk  2 tablespoons

butter

serves  2    takes  1 hour

1 Turn the oven on to 200°C (400°F/Gas 6). Heat the oil in a frying pan, add the onion and carrot and fry them together until they begin to brown around the edges. Add the meat and cook it, turning it over every now and then, mashing out any large lumps with the back of a fork.

2 When the meat is browned all over, add a little flour, about a teaspoon, and stir it in. Add the ketchup and sprinkle on the stock cube. Now add about 250 ml (1 cup) of water and mix everything together. Bring the mixture to the boil, then turn down the heat and simmer gently for about 20 minutes. Season with salt, pepper and Worcestershire sauce.

3 While the meat is cooking, cook the potato in simmering water until the potato chunks are tender (this will take about 12 minutes). When they are soft, drain them and mash them with the milk and plenty of seasoning.

4 Pour the meat into an ovenproof dish or two individual dishes and dollop the potato on top. Dot some butter over the potato and bake (put a baking tray under the dish in case the meat bubbles over the edge of the dish) for about 20 minutes, by which time the top of the potato should be lightly browned. Serve with peas.

# beef

## Why beef?

Beef has a rich flavour that lends itself well to many cooking styles, from 3-minute steaks to slow-cooked casseroles. A good source of protein and iron, beef has a wider range of cuts than any other kind of meat.

## What to look for:

* Beef should be dark red. The longer it has been aged, the darker it will be. Bright red meat is not an indication of quality.

* Beef fat should be creamy in colour and feel firm. Slow cooking joints like brisket, shin, chuck and blade should have veins of fat and sinew running through them as it is these that will make the meat tender.

## How to look after it:

Loose-packed beef can be unwrapped, then put in a container and covered with plastic wrap. Cuts that have been packaged in ridged containers are usually quite sterile and are best left in them until ready for use. Unused raw beef can be tightly wrapped in plastic or freezer bags and frozen for up to 12 months.

## What's available?

* Steaks come in a variety of cuts and you can pretty well choose any one you like for most recipes. Fillet and sirloin steaks don't have bones whereas T-bones do. Be careful not to buy minute steak or sandwich steak unless the recipe specifies it.

* Chuck steak is used for stewing and other methods of slow cooking. It turns very tender after a few hours but it is tough if it is cooked quickly.

* Fillet is either cut into steaks or bought as a whole piece. It roasts quickly (20 minutes) and can be eaten raw as carpaccio (sliced) or steak tartare (minced).

* Rib is sold with bone in or out as a roasting joint and is a lean and tender cut.

* Silverside and topside are used for casseroles, stews and other long-cooking dishes. Like chuck, they will be tough if cooked too quickly.

* Minced (ground) beef is available with various fat contents. Lean mince has less fat but this means it also has less flavour. Some minced beef is finer than others.

# beef ball and white bean soup

minced (ground) beef  300 g (10 oz)

garlic clove  1 crushed

parsley  $1/2$ tablespoon finely chopped

ground cinnamon  a pinch

freshly grated nutmeg  a pinch

egg  1 lightly beaten

beef stock  750 ml (3 cups)

carrot  1 thinly sliced

tinned white beans  400 g (14 oz) drained

Savoy cabbage  $1/4$ finely shredded

Parmesan cheese  freshly grated

serves  2    takes  25 minutes

1 Put the minced beef in a bowl with the garlic, parsley, cinnamon, nutmeg and half of the egg. Mix everything together well and season with salt and pepper. If the mixture is dry, add the rest of the egg — you want it to be sticky enough so that forming small balls is easy.

2 Roll the beef mixture into small balls — they should be small enough to scoop up on a spoon and eat in one mouthful.  Put them on a plate as you make them.

3 Put the beef stock in a saucepan, with the carrot, and bring it to the boil. Add the meatballs, one at a time, and turn the heat down to a simmer. Test one of the balls after 3 minutes. It should be cooked through, so if it isn't, cook them for a little longer. Now add the beans and cabbage and cook for another 4 to 5 minutes. Season the broth to taste.

4 Serve the soup with lots of Parmesan stirred in and plenty of bread to dunk into the broth.

These little meatballs take no time at all to make — it doesn't even matter if they are not particularly round. You can add extra vegetables to the soup base if you like, because it should be quite hearty. Use fresh beef stock if you can, but a tin of beef consommé or ready-made stock sold in cartons will also work.

An absolute classic, this can be served with potatoes and a green salad. You can use whichever cut and size of steak you prefer. Bear in mind that it is better to have a small amount of very good meat.

# steak with maître d'hotel butter

**unsalted butter** 2 tablespoons softened

**parsley** 1 teaspoon finely chopped

**lemon juice**

**steaks** 2, about 1.5 cm (5/8 inch) thick

**olive oil** 1 tablespoon

**serves** 2 **takes** 20 minutes

1 Beat the butter to a cream in a bowl, using a wooden spoon, then beat in a pinch of salt, a pinch of pepper and the parsley. Next add about a teaspoon of lemon juice, a few drops at a time. Let the butter harden in the fridge a little, then form it into a log shape by rolling it up in greaseproof paper. Put it into the fridge until you need it.

2 Season the steaks with salt and pepper on both sides. Heat the oil in a large frying pan and, when it is very hot, add the steaks. Cook them for 2 minutes on each side for rare, 3 minutes on each side for medium, and 4 minutes on each side for well done. The timings may vary depending on the thickness of your steaks — if they are thin, give them a slightly shorter time and if they are thick, cook them for longer.

3 Cut the butter into slices and put a couple of slices on top of each steak. The heat of the steak will melt the butter. Serve with potatoes and vegetables or salad.

This is a delicious salad and is excellent for a summer lunch or supper. Contrasting sweet and sour flavours mixed with the cucumber, and also added to the steak, are a perfect combination.

# beef salad with sweet and sour cucumber

cucumber   1 Lebanese (short)

caster (superfine) sugar   2 teaspoons

red wine vinegar   2 tablespoons

oil   1 tablespoon

fillet steak   1 large or 2 small, cut into strips (150 g/5 oz)

spring onions (scallions)   4 cut into pieces

garlic clove   1 crushed

ginger   1 tablespoon grated

soy sauce   1 tablespoon

mixed lettuce leaves   a couple of handfuls

serves   2   takes   20 minutes

1 Halve the cucumber lengthways, thinly slice it, then put it in a colander. Sprinkle a little bit of salt over it and leave it for about 10 minutes. This will draw out any excess moisture and stop the final flavour from tasting watery. Meanwhile, put 1 teaspoon each of the sugar and the vinegar in a bowl and stir until the sugar dissolves. Rinse the salt off the cucumber and drain the cucumber very thoroughly before dabbing it with a piece of paper towel to soak up any leftover moisture. Mix the cucumber with the vinegar mixture.

2 Heat the oil in a frying pan until it is smoking — this will only take a minute. Add the steak and fry it for a minute, then add the spring onion and fry for another minute. Add the garlic and ginger, toss everything around once, then add the soy sauce and remaining sugar and vinegar. Bubble briefly until the sauce turns sticky.

3 Put a handful of lettuce leaves on two plates and divide the beef between them. Scatter some cucumber on the beef and serve the rest on the side. Any juices will make good salad dressing.

This dish uses chunks of meat, which give it a hearty texture. You must use hot chillies if you want it to be hot in flavour, so choose a Mexican variety such as habanero or jalapeño and add as many as you need. Serve with rice or flour tortillas.

# chilli

black beans or kidney beans   110 g (4 oz)

oil   2 tablespoons

red onion   1 finely chopped

garlic clove   1 crushed

coriander (cilantro)   1 bunch finely chopped

chillies   1 or 2, seeded and finely chopped

chuck steak   800 g (1 lb 12 oz) cut into cubes

tinned chopped tomatoes   400 g (14 oz)

tomato paste (purée)   1 tablespoon

beef stock   1 cup (250 ml)

red capsicum (pepper)   1 cut into squares

ripe tomato   1 chopped

avocado   1/2 diced

lime   1 juiced

sour cream   2 tablespoons

serves 2   takes 2¹/2 hours plus overnight soaking

1 Soak the beans in cold water overnight, or put them in a saucepan, cover with cold water, bring to the boil, then turn down the heat and simmer for 10 minutes. Turn off the heat and leave for 2 hours. Drain and rinse the beans.

2 Heat half of the oil in a large heatproof casserole and gently cook three-quarters of the onion, the garlic, half of the coriander, and the chilli, for 5 minutes.

3 Turn up the heat, push the onion to one side and add the remaining oil. Add the steak and cook it for a couple of minutes, or until it is well browned all over. Add the beans, tomato, tomato paste and stock and stir everything together well. Bring the mixture to the boil, then turn it down to a simmer. Put the lid on and cook it for 1 hour. Add the red capsicum to the casserole, stir it in and cook everything for another 30 minutes.

4 To make the topping, mix half of the remaining coriander, the tomato, avocado and the remaining onion. Season with salt and pepper and add half of the lime juice.

5 When the meat is tender, add the remaining coriander and lime juice and season well. Serve with a portion of the topping spooned over and a dollop of sour cream.

# beef cooked in guinness with celeriac purée

oil   2 tablespoons

chuck steak   1 kg (2 lb 4 oz) cubed

onions   2 chopped

garlic clove   1 crushed

brown sugar   2 teaspoons

plain (all-purpose) flour   2 teaspoons

Guinness   125 ml (1/2 cup)

beef stock   375 ml (1 1/2 cups)

bay leaf   1

thyme   2 sprigs

celeriac   1

potato   1 cubed

milk   250 ml (1 cup)

butter   1 tablespoon

French bread   2 slices toasted

Dijon mustard   1/2 teaspoon

serves  2   takes  2 1/2 hours

1 Put the oven on to 180°C (350°F/Gas 4). Heat half of the oil in a frying pan over a high heat and fry the meat in batches until it is browned all over. Add more oil as you need it. You need to cook the meat in batches so the temperature of the pan stays hot and the meat does not stew. Put the meat in a casserole.

2 Add the onion to the frying pan and fry it gently over a low heat. When the onion starts to turn brown, add the garlic and brown sugar and cook until the onion is fairly brown. Stir in the flour, then transfer to the casserole.

3 Put the Guinness and stock in the frying pan and bring it to the boil, then pour it into the casserole (this will collect any meat juices and flavour from the pan). Add the bay leaf and thyme to the casserole and season well. Bring the whole thing to the boil, put a lid on and put the casserole in the oven for 2 hours.

4 While the casserole is cooking, peel and chop the celeriac. Put the pieces into a bowl of water as you cut them, otherwise they will turn brown. Put the potato and celeriac in a saucepan with the milk and bring to the boil. Cover and cook for 15 minutes, or until the celeriac and potato are tender, then mash everything together with the milk. Season well and add the butter.

5 Spread the French bread with the mustard and serve with the beef ladled over and the celeriac purée on the side.

Although this recipe takes a fair amount of time to cook, there is not a lot of preparation time needed. You can throw a couple of potatoes in the oven when the meat is halfway through cooking and they will be ready to serve at the same time.

Making hamburgers takes no effort, and they taste so much better than bought ones. As these meat patties have no breadcrumbs added, they are fairly solid pieces of meat. If you can't get fresh corn, you can use a small tin of sweet corn instead.

# hamburgers with fresh corn relish

minced (ground) beef  350 g (12 oz)

garlic clove  1

onion  1 very finely chopped

parsley  1 tablespoon finely chopped

tomato ketchup  2 teaspoons

Worcestershire sauce  a few drops

cob of corn  1

tomato  1 finely chopped

sweet chilli sauce  1/2 tablespoon

coriander (cilantro) leaves
a handful

lime juice

oil  1 tablespoon

buns  2

baby cos leaves

serves 2   takes 30 minutes

1 Turn on the grill. Put the beef in a bowl with the garlic, half of the onion, the parsley, tomato ketchup and the Worcestershire sauce. Season and mix well, then leave it to marinate while you make the relish.

2 Grill the corn cob on all sides until it is slightly blackened and charred around the edges. By this time it should be cooked through. Slice off the kernels by slicing down the length of the cob with a sharp knife. Mix the kernels with the tomato, chilli sauce, coriander and remaining onion. Add lime juice and salt and pepper, to taste.

3 Form the beef mixture into two large patties and flatten them out to the size of the buns (bear in mind that they will shrink as they cook).

4 Heat the oil in a frying pan and fry the beef patties for between 3 and 5 minutes on each side, depending on how well cooked you like them. While they are cooking, toast the buns.

5 Lay a lettuce leaf or two on each bun bottom, add some relish and top with a hamburger patty and the bun top. Serve any extra relish on the side.

This makes a very satisfying lunch or supper. If you have a food processor you can chop the herbs really quickly. Minute steaks work well but you can also use fillet. The salsa verde is also a good accompaniment to cold roast beef.

# steak sandwich with salsa verde

garlic clove  1 crushed

parsley  2 handfuls

basil leaves  a handful

mint leaves  a handful

olive oil  2 tablespoons

capers  1 teaspoon chopped

lemon juice  1 teaspoon

red wine vinegar  1 teaspoon

minute steaks  2

ciabatta or Turkish bread  2 chunks halved horizontally

cucumber  8 slices

serves  2    takes  10 minutes

1 To make the salsa verde, put the garlic and herbs in a food processor with half of the oil and whizz them together until they are coarsely chopped. Tip the chopped herbs into a bowl and stir in the capers, lemon juice and vinegar. Season with salt and pepper.

2 Heat the remaining oil in a frying pan and fry the steaks for a minute on each side — they should cook very quickly and start to brown.

3 While the steaks are cooking, toast the bread. Spread some salsa verde on all the pieces of the bread (be generous) and make two sandwiches with the steaks and cucumber.

# potatoes

## Why potatoes?

Potatoes can be eaten as the main feature of a meal, as a side dish, or as a snack, and provided you don't add too much oil or butter to them, they are quite low in fat. Potatoes are rich in vitamin C, as well as being a good source of carbohydrate. Keeping the skin on your potato will give you a more nutritious meal.

## How to look after them:

* Potatoes should be kept in a cool, dark place to stop them turning green or sprouting too quickly. Green potatoes contain mildly poisonous alkaloids, which are indigestible. If you store potatoes in the fridge, they will get sweeter as the starch converts to sugar.

* Ready-washed potatoes may not last as long as ones covered in earth because their protective outer layer has been removed with high pressure jets of water.

## What's available?

Choose potatoes that suit the recipe you are using. Potatoes are not all the same and if you use the wrong sort you won't get the result you want.

* Starchy or mealy potatoes turn fluffy when you cook them. These make good mash, roast potatoes and chips but will crumble when boiled. Look for king edward and russet (idaho).

* Waxy potatoes stay compact and solid. They are good for salads but make really gluey mash. Look for pink fir apple, kipfler, cara and charlotte.

* All-purpose potatoes suit all kinds of recipes. Look for desiree, nicola, spunta and pontiac.

* New potatoes are early variety potatoes, although baby potatoes of all types are sometimes called new potatoes or chats. Look for jersey royals.

Gnocchi made at home are always lighter and more delicious then any you can buy in packets. They are not hard to make — if you can manage mashed potato, it is only one more step to gnocchi.

# chive gnocchi with blue cheese

floury potatoes  450 g (1 lb)

plain (all-purpose) flour
165 g (1$^1$/$_3$ cups)

chives  1 tablespoon chopped

egg yolks  2

blue cheese  50 g (2$^1$/$_2$ tablespoons)

cream  4 tablespoons

serves  2   takes  40 minutes

1 Peel the potatoes and cut them into even-sized pieces. Cook them in simmering water for 20 minutes, or until they are tender. Drain them very well, then mash them in a large bowl. Add 140 g (5 oz) of the flour, the chives and egg yolks, along with some seasoning, and mix everything well. Now add enough of the remaining flour to make a mixture that is soft but not sticky.  Divide the mixture into four, roll each bit into a sausage shape 1 cm ($^1$/$_2$ inch) across and cut off lengths about 1.5 cm ($^5$/$_8$ inch) long. You don't need to shape the gnocchi any more than this.

2 Bring a large saucepan of water to the boil and cook the gnocchi in batches. As it rises to the surface (it will do this when it is cooked through), scoop it out with a slotted spoon and drain it well.

3 While the gnocchi are cooking, put the blue cheese and cream in a saucepan and gently heat them together. Put the gnocchi in a large bowl and pour the blue cheese sauce over it. Gently fold the sauce into the gnocchi and serve.

This is a rather decadent recipe but you can make yourself feel more virtuous by eating it with a salad. Use floury or all-purpose potatoes, as they soak up the milk and cream better than waxy ones.

# individual potato gratins

oil  1 tablespoon

onion  1 finely sliced

garlic clove  1 crushed

floury potatoes  2 large or 4 small

Gruyère cheese  4 tablespoons grated

ground nutmeg  a pinch

milk  80 ml (1/3 cup)

double (thick) cream  80 ml (1/3 cup)

serves  2    takes  1 1/4 hours

1 Put the oven on to 170°C (325°F/Gas 3). Heat the oil in a frying pan over a low heat and add the onion. Stir to coat the onions in oil, then leave to cook until they are completely soft and translucent but not brown. You may need to stir them occasionally to stop them browning in patches. Add the garlic and cook for a minute, then turn off the heat.

2 Thinly slice the potatoes using a sharp knife, making the slices even so they cook at the same rate. Butter two small ovenproof dishes. Equally dividing the ingredients, layer the potato, onion and garlic, grated cheese and nutmeg in the dishes, seasoning as you go. Finish with a layer of potatoes and some cheese. Mix together the milk and cream and divide it between the dishes.

3 Cover the dishes with foil and bake for 10 minutes, then take off the foil and bake for another 40 minutes, or until the potatoes are completely cooked. Test by pushing a sharp knife through the layers to see if the potato still feels hard. If it does, continue cooking. Leave to stand for a few minutes before serving so the sauce soaks into the potatoes.

This recipe makes a great snack and goes particularly well with drinks. Though delicious hot, the potatoes are equally good when cold. They can also be served without the dip.

# roast baby potatoes with sweet chilli dip

**baby potatoes**  12 to 16, depending on size

**olive oil**  1 tablespoon

**thyme leaves**  1 teaspoon

**coarse salt**  1 teaspoon

**sweet chilli sauce**  2 tablespoons

**sour cream**  2 tablespoons

**spring onion (scallion)**  1 finely chopped

**serves**  2    **takes**  40 minutes

1 Put the oven on to 200°C (400°F/Gas 6). If any of your potatoes are too big to eat in more than two bites, cut them in half. Put them in a roasting tin with the oil, thyme and salt and mix them around so they are all coated. Roast for 30 to 40 minutes, or until the potatoes are cooked through.

2 Mix the sweet chilli sauce, sour cream and spring onion together. Serve with the potatoes for dipping.

You can use any blue cheese for this recipe, depending on how strong you would like the final flavour to be. It is worth taking the outer grey skins off the broad beans as the beans are much more tender without them. Baked potatoes are always better if done in the oven but you can use a microwave if you prefer.

# baked potatoes with rocket, broad beans and blue cheese

large potatoes  2

coarse salt

broad beans  a handful (150 g)

cream  2 tablespoons

blue cheese  a handful of crumbled

rocket (arugula)  2 handfuls chopped

serves  2    takes  1 hour 20 minutes

1 Put the oven on to 200°C (400°F/Gas 6). Wash the potatoes and, while they are still damp, rub them with a little salt. Prick them several times and then put them in the oven, sitting directly on the oven shelf. This will help them get a good all-round heat. Bake for 1 hour, then squeeze them gently — they should be soft. If they are still hard, give them another 15 minutes or so.

2 Cook the broad beans in boiling water for 3 minutes, then drain them well. Peel off the outer grey skins.

3 When the potatoes are cooked, cut a cross in one side of each and squeeze the potatoes around the middle until they open up.

4 Put the cream in a small saucepan, add the broad beans, cook them gently for a minute or two, then add the blue cheese and rocket. Stir everything together and when the rocket has wilted, spoon the mixture into the potatoes. Season with black pepper.

These bubble and squeak cakes are a deliciouly easy supper, and if you have leftover potatoes and cabbage you can make them very quickly. If not, it is worth starting from scratch. You could also top each of the cakes with a fried or poached egg instead of the bacon if you prefer. Use a non-stick frying pan if you have one.

# cheesy bubble and squeak cakes with bacon

floury potatoes  2 large or 4 small

milk  1 tablespoon

butter  1 tablespoon

Savoy cabbage  3 handfuls of shredded

Cheddar cheese  a handful of grated

oil  1 tablespoon

bacon rashers  4, rinds cut off

serves  2    takes  30 minutes

1 Cut the potatoes into pieces and cook them in simmering water for 15 minutes, or until they are soft. Drain them well, put them back in the pan with the milk and mash them until they are smooth. Season with salt and pepper.

2 Melt the butter in a non-stick frying pan and cook the cabbage until it is soft. Add this to the potato along with the cheese. The mixture should be stiff enough to form the potato into cakes — it is up to you whether you make large ones or small ones.

3 Heat the oil in the same frying pan over a medium heat and cook the bacon on both sides until it is crisp. Push it to one side, then add the potato cakes. Fry them on both sides until they are well browned and slightly crisp. Shake the pan occasionally to move the cakes around so they don't stick. Serve the bubble and squeak cakes with the bacon.

# tomatoes

## Why tomatoes?

Tomatoes can be used both as a main ingredient and as a flavouring. They are equally good eaten raw or cooked and they add both colour and flavour to dishes.

## What to look for:

It is virtually impossible to tell how good a tomato is until you taste it. However, choosing ripe-looking tomatoes that actually smell of tomato should improve your chance of getting good ones.

## How to look after them:

If your tomatoes aren't ripe when you bring them home, leave them on the bench to ripen. You can keep them in the fridge once they are ripe but they taste better if you eat them at room temperature.

## What's available?

You can buy red, yellow, orange and, sometimes, pink tomatoes. Choose a colour that will suit your recipe or mix several colours.

* Roma (plum) tomatoes are good for soups and sauces as they have a concentrated flavour when cooked.

* Beefsteak tomatoes are larger tomatoes, which are particularly good for making stuffed tomatoes.

* Cherry and grape tomatoes are tiny tomatoes good for snacking on, roasting, and tossing into salads.

* Ordinary round tomatoes are usually good for salads and can be used for cooking as well.

* Vine-ripened tomatoes come attached to their vine. They often have a more 'tomatoey' flavour.

Ciabatta works particularly well for bruschetta as it turns very crisp when toasted. However, you can use any good-quality crusty bread. Eat your bruschetta as soon as you have made it because, if you leave it to sit, the juice from the tomatoes may make it go soggy.

# tomato and pesto bruschetta

ciabatta  4 thick slices

olive oil  2 tablespoons

fresh pesto  3 tablespoons

ripe Roma (plum) tomatoes  4

mascarpone cheese  2 tablespoons

serves  2    takes  15 minutes

1 Turn the grill to its highest setting. Brush both sides of each piece of bread with olive oil and put the bread on a baking tray. Grill for 3 minutes on each side, or until crisp and golden brown.

2 Spread a teaspoon of pesto over each piece of bruschetta and take them off the tray. Slice the tomatoes into four pieces lengthways and drain them for a minute on a piece of paper towel — this will stop the juice from the tomatoes making the bruschetta soggy. Put the tomato slices on the baking tray.

3 Grill the tomato for about 5 minutes, by which time it will start to cook and brown at the edges. When the tomato is cooked, layer four slices onto each piece of bruschetta. Put the bruschetta back on the tray and grill it for another minute to heat it through. Add a dollop of mascarpone and a little more pesto to each bruschetta and serve hot.

This Italian salad is a good one to make ahead of time. It tastes even better the next day when the flavours have had time to develop. It can be eaten on its own, served with barbecued or grilled meat or fish, or tossed through hot pasta to make an instant sauce.

# tomato caponata with mozzarella

small eggplant (aubergine)  1 cubed

olive oil

onion  1/2 cubed

celery stalk  1 sliced

red capsicum (pepper)  1/2 cubed

ripe Roma (plum) tomatoes  2 chopped

cherry tomatoes  8 red and 8 yellow, cut in halves

red wine vinegar  1 tablespoon

sugar  a pinch

capers  1 tablespoon rinsed

black olives  8 unpitted

mozzarella cheese  200 g (7 oz) ball chopped

parsley  a handful roughly chopped

serves 2   takes 35 minutes

1 Cook the eggplant in boiling salted water for a minute, then drain it. Squeeze out any excess moisture with your hands. This pre-cooking stops the eggplant from soaking up too much oil.

2 Heat a tablespoon of olive oil in a large frying pan and add the eggplant. Brown on all sides over a high heat, adding more oil if you need to. When the eggplant is cooked, take it out and drain it on paper towels.

3 Add a little more oil to the pan, turn down the heat and cook the onion and celery for about 5 minutes, or until soft but not brown. Add the red capsicum and cook it for 2 minutes. Add the chopped tomato and a tablespoon of water. Simmer the mixture for 5 minutes, or until the mixture is quite dry, then stir in the cherry tomatoes.

4 Season the mixture well with black pepper. Add the red wine vinegar, sugar, capers and olives and cook everything for 2 to 3 minutes over a low heat. Add the drained eggplant and cook it for 5 minutes. Take the mixture off the heat and leave it to cool. Toss the mozzarella and parsley through the caponata and serve it with a green salad and some bread to mop up the juices.

One of the original pizzas from Naples and still one of the yummiest. You can use a bought pizza base or make one using a packet mix, depending on how much time you have. Most supermarkets now sell decent ready-made bases. You need one about 30 cm (12 inches) across.

# pizza margherita

pizza base mix  1 packet, or a ready-made base

very ripe Roma (plum) tomatoes  4

basil leaves  12

garlic cloves  2 crushed

passata  1 tablespoon

olive oil  4 tablespoons

mozzarella cheese  200 g (7 oz) ball chopped

makes  1 large    takes  1 hour, depending on proving time

1 If you are using a packet mix, make up the pizza base following the instructions on the packet and leave it to prove. Heat the oven to as high as it will go — pizzas should cook as quickly as possible.

2 Take the cores, seeds and juices out of the tomatoes, chop the tomatoes roughly, then purée them in a food processor with 4 basil leaves (if you don't have a food processor, chop the tomatoes and basil very finely and stir them together). Stir in the garlic, passata and 2 tablespoons of olive oil and season well.

3 Roll out the pizza base to a 30 cm (12 inch) circle and put it on an oiled baking tray — if it shrinks when you move it, just stretch it out again. Drizzle it with a little of the olive oil. Spoon the tomato sauce over the base, spreading it up to the rim. Scatter the mozzarella over the top and drizzle with a little more olive oil.

4 Cook the pizza for 2 to 12 minutes (this will depend on how hot your oven is), or until the base is light brown and crisp and the topping is cooked. Before serving, drizzle with a little more oil and scatter the remaining basil over the top.

# eggplants

## Why eggplants?

Eggplants, or aubergines, appear in many cuisines and come in a variety of shapes, colours and sizes. Eggplants can be bitter, a trait that is not valued in some recipes but is used as a flavouring in others such as Thai curries. Eggplants are nearly always eaten cooked, though smaller types are sometimes used raw in Asian dishes.

## What to look for:

Choose shiny, plump eggplants that feel heavy for their size. Avoid any with brown patches or wrinkles.

## How to use them:

Recipes often call for eggplants to be salted (degorged) and left to drain in a colander. This draws out any bitter juices they may have. Commercially grown eggplants tend not to be as bitter as they were in the past, but salting them also helps stop them soaking up too much oil.

Eggplants soak up lots of oil while they are cooking. To make them less spongelike, blanch them for a minute or two in boiling water before cooking them.

## What's available?

* Large purple eggplants are good for stuffing, baking whole or slicing. They are mild in flavour.

* Long Asian eggplants are good for slicing into rounds and using for stir-fries and kebabs.

* Small, round, white or pale green eggplants are good for halving or quartering and using in Asian, especially Thai, dishes. They are slightly more bitter than the purple eggplants.

* Tiny green pea eggplants are used whole in Thai recipes. They are the most tart and bitter in flavour of all the eggplants.

# spiced eggplant

eggplant (aubergine)  1 sliced

onion  1 finely chopped

ginger  1 cm (1/2 inch) piece grated

garlic cloves  2 crushed

red chilli  1 finely chopped

tinned tomatoes  250 g (1 cup)

oil  for frying

ground turmeric  1/4 teaspoon

kalonji  1/4 teaspoon

garam masala  1 teaspoon

coriander (cilantro)  a handful chopped


serves  2    takes  40 minutes

1 Put the eggplant slices in a colander, sprinkle them with salt and leave them for 30 minutes — this will draw out any bitter juices. Rinse the slices and squeeze them well to get rid of any excess water, then pat them dry with paper towels.

2 Mix the onion, ginger, garlic and chilli with the tomatoes. If you have a blender or food processor, give them a quick whizz in that, but if not, just finely chop the tomatoes first and stir them together.

3 Heat a little oil in a large, deep heavy-based frying pan and, when it is hot, add as many eggplant slices as you can fit in a single layer. Cook them over a medium heat until they are browned on both sides, then drain them in a sieve to get rid of any excess oil. Cook the rest of the eggplant in batches, using as much oil as you need and draining off the excess.

4 Heat a tablespoon of oil in the frying pan, add the turmeric, kalonji and garam masala and stir for a few seconds, then add the tomato. Cook, stirring for 5 minutes, or until the mixture thickens (be careful as the mixture tends to spit when it gets thick). Carefully add the cooked eggplant so the slices stay whole, cover the pan and cook gently for about 10 minutes. Season with salt to taste and stir the coriander through.

This recipe can be eaten as a main course with rice or couscous, or served as a vegetable accompaniment to curries or grilled meats. To make it hotter, use more chilli. Kalonji are also called nigella seeds or black cumin and are sold in Indian food shops and some supermarkets.

A classic Turkish dish, the name means the imam (priest) fainted — presumably because the dish was so delicious. You can serve this hot, warm or cold and it will keep well if you want to make it the day before. It goes well with rice or couscous.

# imam bayildi

eggplant (aubergine)  1

olive oil  3 tablespoons

medium onion  1 chopped

garlic clove  1 crushed

ripe tomatoes  3 chopped

ground cinnamon  1/2 teaspoon

parsley  a handful chopped

tomato juice  250 ml (1 cup)

thick natural yoghurt

serves  2  takes  1 hour 20 minutes

1 Put the oven on to 200°C (400°F/Gas 6). Cut the eggplant in half lengthways. To hollow out the middle, run a small sharp knife around edge of the cut half, about 1 cm (1/2 inch) from the skin — don't go through too far or you will cut through the bottom skin. Dig out the flesh in the middle, within the cut line, to leave two shells. Keep the flesh and chop it finely.

2 Heat 2 tablespoons of the oil in a frying pan and fry the eggplant flesh, onion and garlic until the onion is soft and cooked through. Add the chopped tomato and any juices and stir everything together. Season with salt and pepper and add the cinnamon. Cook the mixture until it is dryish, then stir in the parsley.

3 Fill the eggplant shells with the mixture and put them in a baking dish. Pour the tomato juice around the eggplant — this will help stop the eggplant drying out as it cooks. Drizzle with the remaining oil.

4 Bake the eggplant shells for 1 hour, by which time the flesh should be tender and the filling browned on top. Serve with some of the tomato juice spooned over and a dollop of yoghurt on top.

Serve this on its own with pitta bread, or with grilled chicken pieces, or toss it through pasta as an interesting sauce. Use fresh ricotta if you can, rather than the stuff in tubs, as it is firmer and has a fresher flavour.

# grilled eggplant with ricotta and tomato

**eggplant (aubergine)** 1 sliced

**olive oil** 2 tablespoons

**cherry tomatoes** 250 g (9 oz) halved

**garlic clove** 1 crushed

**capers** 1 teaspoon drained

**ricotta** 3 tablespoons

**basil leaves** a few small

**serves** 2   **takes** 20 minutes

1 Heat the grill to high. Brush the eggplant slices with some of the oil. Grill the slices on both sides until they are brown, then lay them in a small shallow baking dish (choose one that will fit under the grill).

2 Heat the rest of the oil in a small saucepan, tip in the cherry tomatoes and garlic, then fry briefly until the tomatoes just start to soften. Add the capers for a minute. Tip the tomatoes over the eggplant, season well and spoon the ricotta on top. Put the dish back under the grill until the ricotta starts to bubble, then scatter the basil over the top.

spinach

## Why spinach?

If cartoons are to be believed, then Popeye's diet of spinach is something to be emulated. Spinach contains iron and vitamins A and C but, on the downside, it also contains oxalic acid, which inhibits their absorption — which means Popeye wasn't just eating spinach! Spinach is just as good raw or cooked and has a simple fresh flavour.

## What to look for:

Choose spinach that is perky looking and buy it in bunches, rather than in plastic bags, if possible. Spinach is best when very fresh so buy it as you need it.

## How to cook it:

* Cook spinach in a minimum amount of water: steaming or wilting is best. If you are using cooked spinach for a recipe, squeeze it dry first or it will dilute whatever you are adding it to.

* Bear in mind that a large pile of spinach leaves will cook down to almost nothing — you'll need about 225 g (7 oz) per person.

## What's available?

* Spinach, sometimes called English spinach, has rounded leaves when small (baby) and more pointed, jagged or curly leaves when older.

* Silverbeet, or Swiss chard, which is called spinach in Australia, has whiter, thick fleshy stems, coarser, crinkled leaves and a stronger flavour.

* New Zealand spinach, also called warrigal greens and tetragon, is not true spinach but can be cooked in the same way. It is at its best when young.

You can use fresh or frozen spinach for this dish, depending on what you have to hand. If you use frozen spinach, one box will be enough. This recipe is delicious for breakfast, topped with a poached egg, or served for lunch or dinner tossed through pasta or noodles, or as a vegetable accompaniment.

# spinach with garlic and chilli

baby spinach leaves  250 g (9 oz)

olive oil  2 tablespoons

garlic clove  1 crushed

red chilli  1 finely chopped

cream  2 tablespoons

cayenne pepper

serves 2   takes 15 minutes

1 Wash the spinach thoroughly and shake it dry, leaving a little water clinging to the leaves. If you are using frozen spinach, defrost it thoroughly and drain it very well — squeeze it with your hands to get rid of excess moisture.

2 Heat the oil in a frying pan, add the garlic and chilli and cook them for a few seconds, being careful not to burn them. Add the spinach and stir it through the oil. Put a lid on the pan for a minute to create some steam. Remove the lid and turn up the heat. Stir the spinach, turning it over frequently until all the liquid has evaporated, then season well. Drizzle with the cream and dust with cayenne pepper.

Baby spinach leaves are best for this as they are more tender. You can use leftover chicken from a roast or simply buy a piece of roasted chicken. This recipe also works well if you replace the tahini, sesame oil and sesame seeds with peanut butter, ordinary oil and peanuts.

# spinach salad with chicken and sesame dressing

**baby spinach leaves**  225 g (8 oz)

**cucumber**  an 8 cm (3 inch) piece peeled and diced

**spring onions (scallions)**  2 shredded

**carrot**  1 cut into matchsticks

**chicken**  1 cooked breast

**tahini**  1 tablespoon

**lime juice**  1 tablespoon

**sesame oil**  2 teaspoons

**sugar**  1/2 teaspoon

**chilli flakes**  a small pinch

**sesame seeds**  1 tablespoon

**coriander (cilantro) leaves**  a small handful

**serves**  2   **takes**  25 minutes

1 Put the spinach in a large bowl. Scatter the cucumber, spring onion and carrot over the top.

2 Shred the chicken breast into long pieces and scatter it over the vegetables.

3 Mix together the tahini, lime juice, sesame oil, sugar and chilli flakes, then add salt to taste. Drizzle this dressing over the salad.

4 Cook the sesame seeds in a dry frying pan over a low heat for a minute or two, stirring them around. When they start to brown and smell toasted, tip them over the salad. Scatter the coriander leaves over the top. Toss the salad just before serving.

Frittata can be eaten hot with a salad and some bread. However, it is also good made into a sandwich using Turkish bread and a relish — the perfect picnic food, in fact.

# spinach and zucchini frittata

olive oil  1 tablespoon

red onion  1/2 thinly sliced

zucchini (courgette)  1 sliced

garlic clove  1 crushed

baby spinach leaves  150 g (5 1/2 oz), stalks removed

eggs  3

cream  1 tablespoon

Emmenthal cheese  40 g (1/3 cup) grated

serves  2    takes  25 minutes

1 Heat the oil in a frying pan and fry the onion and zucchini over a medium heat until they are a pale golden brown. Add the garlic and cook it for a minute. Add the spinach and cook until the spinach has wilted and any excess moisture has evaporated off — if you don't do this, your frittata will end up soggy in the middle, as the liquid will continue to come out as it cooks. Shake the pan so you get an even layer of mixture. Turn the heat down to low.

2 Beat the eggs and cream together and season with salt and pepper. Stir in half of the cheese and pour the mixture over the spinach. Cook the bottom of the frittata for about 4 minutes, or until the egg is just set. While you are doing this, turn on the grill. When the bottom of the frittata is set, scatter on the rest of the cheese and put the frying pan under the grill to cook the top.

3 Turn the frittata out of the frying pan after leaving it to set for a minute. Cut it into quarters to serve.

# mushrooms

## Why mushrooms?

Mushrooms can be used both as a flavouring and as the main part of a dish. There is a huge assortment of varieties, although if you only shop at supermarkets, you'll be restricted in choice. Don't ever pick wild mushrooms unless you know exactly what type they are — there are lots of poisonous types.

## What to look for:

Mushrooms should feel firm and look fresh. Caps should be smooth and undamaged and gills should be unsquashed. If the stalks are shrunken, the mushrooms were picked some time ago and are beginning to dry out.

## How to look after them:

Refrigerate mushrooms in paper bags as plastic ones make them sweat. Before using mushrooms, wipe them rather than washing them as they absorb water like sponges.

## What's available?

* Large field or flat mushrooms can be treated almost like steak. They have a firm texture and have more flavour than button mushrooms so they are good for soups.

* Button mushrooms have a delicate flavour but stand up well to cooking. They come in varying sizes, some with a slightly open cap.

* Oyster mushrooms come in pale brownish grey, yellow and pink. They have a pretty shape and delicate flavour and need to be cooked gently.

* Wild mushrooms come in a wide variety of shapes and sizes. Porcini, or ceps, are most easily available dried and have a strong, earthy flavour. Wild mushrooms add interest to any mushroom dish so, if they are available, use them instead of button mushrooms.

* Shiitake mushrooms are available fresh as well as dried. They go very well with Asian flavours but can be used successfully in any mixed mushroom dish.

* Asian mushrooms such as shimeji and enoki are quite delicate and need to be cooked only for the briefest time. Toss them into stir-fries right at the end or use them as garnishes.

Mushroom soup does not always look appetizing because of the colour — the flavour, however, is divine. If you make the soup with field mushrooms, you will get a much darker colour and richer flavour than you will using button mushrooms. If you don't want a creamy style soup, simply serve the soup with a dollop of cream as a garnish.

# mushroom soup

butter  1 tablespoon

onion  1/2 finely chopped

large field mushrooms  6 finely chopped (about 700 g/1 lb 9 oz)

garlic clove  1 crushed

dry sherry  1 tablespoon

chicken or vegetable stock  500 ml (2 cups)

parsley  1 tablespoon finely chopped

cream

serves  2   takes  30 minutes

1 Melt the butter in a saucepan and fry the onion until the onion is translucent but not browned. Add the chopped mushroom and the garlic and continue frying. Initially the mushrooms might give off a lot of liquid, so keep frying until it is all absorbed back into the mixture. This will take 10–12 minutes.

2 Add the sherry to the pan, turn up the heat and let the mixture bubble — this burns off the alcohol but leaves the flavour. Cool slightly, then transfer to a blender. Whizz together until a smooth paste forms, then add the stock and blend until smooth. Add the parsley and a couple of tablespoons of cream and blend together. Pour back into the saucepan and heat gently. Serve with bread.

Big field mushrooms are almost meaty in texture. In this recipe they are grilled whole, with garlic, chilli and parsley in the middle, and basted with butter. Eat them on toast as here, with potatoes or pasta, or as a vegetarian alternative to steak.

# grilled field mushrooms with garlic and chilli

field mushrooms  2 large or 4 medium

butter  1 tablespoon softened

garlic clove  1 crushed

small red chilli  1 finely chopped

parsley  2 tablespoons finely chopped

ciabatta  2 thick slices

tomato chutney or relish

crème fraîche

serves  2    takes  15 minutes

1 Put the grill on and cover the grill rack with a piece of foil so any juices stay with the mushrooms as they cook. Gently pull the stalks out of the mushrooms and peel off the skins if they are dirty.

2 Mix together the butter, garlic, chilli and parsley and spread some over the inside of each mushroom. Make sure the butter is quite soft so it spreads easily. Season well.

3 Grill the mushrooms under a medium heat for about 8 minutes — they need to be cooked right through. Test the centres with the point of a knife if you are not sure.

4 Toast the bread, spread some tomato chutney or relish on each slice, then top with a mushroom (or two) and serve straight away. A dollop of crème fraîche will make the whole dish even more decadent.

The flavour of dried porcini will enhance that of the fresh mushrooms. You can buy porcini in small packets from delis and some supermarkets — one packet will easily be enough.

# porcini and walnut pasta

porcini   10 g (¹/₄ oz) or 1 small packet

penne   200 g (7 oz)

olive oil   1 tablespoon

onion   ¹/₂ finely chopped

garlic clove   1 crushed

button mushrooms   about 12, sliced

thyme sprigs   2

walnuts   a handful

sour cream   1 tablespoon

Parmesan cheese   freshly grated

serves   2    takes   35 minutes

1 Put the porcini in a bowl with just enough boiling water to cover them and leave to soak for half an hour. If they soak up all the water quickly, add a little more. Chop if the pieces are large.

2 Cook the penne in a large saucepan of boiling salted water until it is *al dente*, stirring once or twice to make sure the pieces are not stuck together. The cooking time will vary, depending on the brand of pasta you have bought. Check the pasta occasionally as it cooks because packet instructions are often too long by a minute or two.

3 Heat the oil in a deep frying pan and fry the onion and garlic together until translucent but not browned. Add the porcini and any soaking liquid, mushrooms and thyme, and keep frying. The mushrooms will give off liquid as they cook so keep cooking until they soak it back up again.

4 In a separate pan, fry the walnuts without any oil until they start to brown and smell toasted. When they have cooled down a bit, roughly chop them and add them to the frying pan. Toss with the drained penne, stir the sour cream through and season well. Serve with the Parmesan.

# tofu

# Why tofu?

Much maligned and often misunderstood, tofu, or bean curd, is a very versatile ingredient. Although tofu has a bland flavour, it takes on other flavourings very well. It is high in protein, low in fat and has lots of vitamins B and E. Tofu has a variety of textures, from soft and slippery to porous and spongy. Choose a texture that suits the dish you are making.

# What to look for:

* Made from soy beans, tofu is a white cheeselike curd that comes in varying degrees of softness, depending on how much water has been pressed out of it. Use firm tofu for robust cooking methods such as stir-frying. Softer tofus are used for soups.

# How to look after it:

* Store tofu in a bowl of cold water in the fridge for up to 5 days and change the water daily.

# What's available?

* Soft (silken) tofu is very delicate and is usually used in soups, or cooked by gentle methods such as steaming.

* Silken firm tofu is slightly more robust and can be fried or grilled successfully.

* Firm tofu is very firm in texture and because it is more robust it can be stir-fried easily without breaking up.

* Deep-fried tofu puffs can be used whole or chopped up in soups, stir-fries and braised dishes. Their porous texture is good at soaking up sauces.

* Sheets or skin, sometimes called yuba, can be shredded and added to stir-fries and soups, or can be used whole as wrappers.

This is a classic Japanese recipe and it is very easy to make once you've sourced the ingredients. All the ingredients can be bought from Japanese food shops and are now in many supermarkets as well. Use light soy sauce for a paler broth.

# agedashi tofu

silken firm tofu  250 g (9 oz) or 1 packet

cornflour (cornstarch)  1 tablespoon

oil  for deep-frying

dashi granules  1¹/₂ teaspoons

soy sauce  2 teaspoons

spring onion (scallion)  1 finely sliced

ginger  1 teaspoon grated

bonito flakes

serves 2    takes 10 minutes

1 Cut the tofu into cubes, dust it with the cornflour and shake off any excess.

2 Fill a saucepan one-third full with oil and heat it over a high heat until the oil reaches 180°C (350°F). If you don't have a thermometer, you can tell the temperature by frying a cube of bread — the oil is ready if it only takes 10 seconds to brown the bread. If it takes longer, keep heating the oil, and if it takes a shorter time, turn off the heat and allow the oil to cool down a little.

3 Deep-fry the tofu in batches until it is golden all over, then drain it well, first in a sieve and then on paper towels.

4 Put 250 ml (1 cup) water in a saucepan, add the dashi granules and soy sauce and bring the mixture to the boil.

5 Divide the tofu between two bowls and sprinkle on the spring onion and ginger. Pour the dashi mixture over the tofu and garnish each bowl with a pinch of bonito flakes.

Tofu has a bland flavour that lends itself to being teamed with strongly flavoured sauces such as soy and oyster sauces. You can add any kind of vegetables to this recipe — baby corn and bamboo shoots go particularly well.

# stir-fried tofu with oyster sauce

firm tofu  250 g (9 oz)

oil  2 tablespoons

garlic clove  1 crushed

ginger  1 teaspoon grated

oyster sauce  1 tablespoon

soy sauce  1 tablespoon

sugar  1 teaspoon

oyster mushrooms  4 quartered

spring onion  1 cut into pieces

baby bok choy  1 quartered

coriander (cilantro) leaves  a handful

serves 2  takes 20 minutes

1 Cut the tofu into bite-sized pieces. Heat a wok over a medium heat, add the oil and heat it until it is very hot and almost smoking. Cook the tofu until it is golden brown on all sides, making sure you move it around gently or it will stick and break.

2 Add the garlic, ginger, oyster sauce, soy sauce and sugar, then toss until well combined. Add the oyster mushrooms, spring onion and bok choy, then simmer until the sauce has reduced a little and the spring onion and bok choy have softened slightly. Garnish with coriander leaves.

Silken tofu can be quite hard to handle as it is very soft, so be gentle with it. In this recipe it is left cold and is heated by pouring hot oil over it at the end. The texture should be cool and slippery. This dish goes very well with steaming hot rice.

# silken tofu with chilli and spring onion

silken tofu   250 g (9 oz)

spring onions   2 thinly sliced

red chilli   1 finely chopped

coriander (cilantro)   a handful roughly chopped

sweet chilli sauce   1 tablespoon

soy sauce   2 tablespoons

oil   2 tablespoons

sesame oil   1 teaspoon

serves   2   takes   10 minutes

1 Open the tofu and drain off any excess liquid. Cut the tofu into cubes and put it on a heatproof plate.

2 Scatter the spring onion, chilli, coriander, sweet chilli sauce and soy sauce over the tofu.

3 Put the oils in a small saucepan and heat them until they are smoking hot, then immediately pour the oils over the tofu and its garnishes.

# chocolate

## Why chocolate?

An object of obsession and a panacea, chocolate has a wonderfully rich flavour and a smooth texture, which makes it ideal for cooking. Chocolate comes in different percentages of cocoa butter and is also available in milk and white.

## What to look for:

* Buy the type of chocolate the recipe asks for. Using a different type may change the recipe as chocolates vary in fat and sugar content.

* For the best flavour, buy good-quality chocolate with a high cocoa butter content, at least fifty per cent.

## How to use it:

* To melt chocoate, chop it finely and put it in a bowl over a pan of simmering water (without letting the bowl touch the water). Leave the chocolate to soften, then stir it until smooth. Moisture will make chocolate seize (turn into a thick mass that won't melt) so be careful not to let any liquid come into contact with it.

* To microwave chocolate, put the chopped chocolate in a bowl and heat it for a couple of minutes. Keep watching and as soon as it starts to look glossy, take it out and stir it.

## What's available?

* Couverture chocolate has a high percentage of cocoa butter and needs to be tempered (heated and cooled) before use. It melts and coats easily, has a glossy finish and an intense chocolate flavour. It is usually sold in catering sized blocks.

* White chocolate is made from cocoa butter and milk solids and is not strictly chocolate as it doesn't contain cocoa liquor. Treat it with care as it will seize more easily than dark chocolate. Not all recipes work with white instead of dark chocolate.

* Cooking chocolate usually contains vegetable fat instead of cocoa butter and doesn't have the same depth of flavour as dark chocolate. Chocolate chips and buttons are made of this.

* Dark, semi-sweet and bitter-sweet chocolate have vanilla, sugar and cocoa butter added to them. Their sugar content and flavour varies but they are all good for cooking. Good-quality dark chocolate is glossy, smooth and slightly red in colour. It snaps cleanly, melts easily and has a sweet, almost fruity smell.

* Milk chocolate has milk solids added to it. It is sweet and creamy and not as intensely chocolate-flavoured as dark chocolate.

# chocolate pudding

dark chocolate  80 g (3 oz) chopped

butter  for greasing

caster (superfine) sugar  40 g (1¹/₂ oz)

milk chocolate  30 g (1 oz) chopped

eggs  2

cream

serves  2    takes  40 minutes

1 Put the oven on to 200°C (400°F/Gas 6). Put the dark chocolate in a glass bowl and set it above a pan of simmering water. (Don't let the bottom of the bowl actually touch the water or it will get too hot.) The chocolate will gradually start to soften and look glossy — when it does this, stir it until it is smooth.

2 Rub a little butter around the inside of two 200 ml (7 fl oz) ramekins. Add ¹/₂ teaspoon of the sugar to each and shake it around until the insides are coated. Divide the chopped milk chocolate between the ramekins.

3 Whisk the rest of the sugar with the egg yolks, using electric beaters, for about 2 minutes, or until you have a pale, creamy mass. You can do this by hand but it will take longer. Clean the beaters and dry them thoroughly — if you don't do this your egg whites won't thicken when you whisk them. Whisk the egg whites until they are thick enough to stand up in peaks.

4 Fold the melted chocolate into the yolk mixture and then fold in the whites. Use a large spoon or rubber spatula to do this and try not to squash out too much air. Divide the mixture between the two ramekins. Bake for 15 minutes. The puddings should be puffed and spongelike. Serve straight away with cream or ice cream.

These puddings are almost like soufflés when cooked — hot, fluffy and very chocolaty. Serve them with cold cream or ice cream to cut through the richness.

This is one of the easiest puddings you can make
— provided you can make a good shot of espresso
or coffee. If you prefer, you can just buy a good
chocolate ice cream, then proceed from step 4.
You can also use vanilla ice cream.

# chocolate affogato

dark chocolate  110 g (4 oz)

milk  500 ml (2 cups)

eggs  3

caster (superfine) sugar  55 g (1/4 cup)

thick (double) cream  170 ml (2/3 cup)

coffee  2 small cups of espresso or very strong

Frangelico or any other liqueur that you like  2 shots

serves  2  takes  a day for the ice cream and 5 minutes to assemble

1 Break the chocolate into individual squares and put it with the milk in a saucepan. Heat the milk over low heat — you must do this slowly or the chocolate will catch on the bottom. As the milk heats up and the chocolate melts, stir the mixture until you have a smooth liquid. You don't need to boil the milk, as the chocolate will melt at a much lower temperature.

2 Whisk the eggs and sugar together with a balloon whisk or electric beaters, in a large glass or metal bowl, until the mixture is pale and frothy. Add the milk and chocolate mixture, along with the cream, and mix.

3 Pour the mixture into a plastic or metal (metal freezes faster) container and put it in the freezer. In order to make a smooth ice cream you will now have to whisk the mixture every hour or so to break up the ice crystals as they form. The more you do this, the smoother your ice cream will be. If you don't do it, all your ice cream will have an icy texture. When the mixture gets very stiff, leave it to set overnight.

4 Scoop two balls of ice cream out of the container and put them into two small cups, then put these in the freezer while you make the coffee. Make the coffee.

5 Serve the ice cream with the Frangelico and coffee poured over it. Eat the rest of the ice cream within the next week for it to be at its best.

These are the smoothest, richest little puddings ever. You must use the best white chocolate you can find — and that means the expensive stuff. The quality not only affects the flavour — if you use cheap white chocolate the recipe may not work at all. Make these in espresso-sized cups and serve them with coffee.

# white chocolate creams

thick (double) cream   250 ml (1 cup)

cardamom pods   4 slightly crushed

bay leaf   1

white chocolate   150 g (5$^{1}$/$_{2}$ oz)

egg yolks   3

serves   4 (or 2 if you are greedy)

takes   4 hours including setting

1 Put the cream, cardamom and bay leaf in a saucepan and gently bring the mixture to the boil. Leave it to one side so the cardamom and bay leaf flavours infuse into the cream.

2 Grate or finely chop the white chocolate — this will make it melt much faster and also lessen the chance of it all going lumpy — and put it in a bowl. Gently heat the cream up again until it is almost boiling and then pour it through a sieve (to strain out the cardamom and bay leaf) over the chocolate. Stir until the chocolate has dissolved. Gently whisk the egg yolks and stir them into the mixture.

3 Pour the mixture into four espresso cups or really small bowls and put them in the fridge to set. They should be ready in a couple of hours if you don't keep opening the fridge door to look at them.

If you are going to eat something that is deliciously bad for you, you may as well do it with a vengeance. The chocolate chips can be milk, plain or white — or a mixture. You will need a cake tin — a 20 x 15 cm (8 x 6 inch) one would be perfect but any old one roughly that size will do. Just remember, the bigger the tin the thinner your brownies will be and vice versa.

# double chocolate brownies

butter  80 g (about 4 tablespoons)

cocoa powder  40 g (1/3 cup)

caster (superfine) sugar  145 g (2/3 cup)

eggs  2

plain (all-purpose) flour  60 g (1/2 cup)

baking powder  1/2 teaspoon

chocolate chips  100 g (1/2 cup)

makes  12    takes  40 minutes

1 Put the oven on to 180°C (350°F/Gas 4). Brush your cake tin with oil or melted butter, put a piece of baking paper in the bottom (at a pinch you can use your butter wrapper if it is not a metallic one).

2 Melt the butter in a saucepan but don't walk away while you are doing this or you may end up with brown or burnt butter. When it is ready, take it off the heat and stir in the cocoa and sugar, followed by the eggs.

3 Put a sieve over the saucepan and tip in the flour and baking powder, along with a pinch of salt. Sift everything into the saucepan, then mix it in. Make sure you don't have any pockets of flour. Add the chocolate chips and stir them in.

4 Pour the mixture into your tin and bake it for 30 minutes. If you have used a different sized tin, the cooking time may be shorter (bigger tin) or longer (smaller tin). You will know your brownies are cooked when you can poke a skewer or knife into the middle of them and it comes out clean. Remember though, the chocolate chips may have melted and if your skewer hits one of those, it might look as if the mixture is still wet. Leave the slab to cool in the tin, then tip it out and cut it into brownie pieces.

cream

## Why cream?

Cream is not an evil ingredient despite its high fat content. Cream adds 'mouthfeel' and a creamy lightness to dishes and provided you don't live on the stuff it won't hurt you. It also contains lots of vitamin A.

## What to look for:

Real cream comes in a variety of thicknesses, depending on its butterfat content, and varies in colour from yellow to white (depending on what the cow has been eating). Cream in a squirty can is not real cream.

* When you want to whip cream you will need to choose a variety that has more than 35% butterfat — single or light creams won't do.

* If you whip cream by hand you are less likely to turn it into butter by mistake. As soon as the cream thickens enough to stick to the whisk, stop whisking. Chilling the whisk and bowl will help the process.

## What's available?

* Single cream has about 18% butterfat. It won't whip but is used for pouring or stirring into soups.

* Whipping cream has 35% butterfat and is used specifically for whipping as it gives a light result.

* Cream has 35% butterfat and is used for whipping. It is thick enough to spoon over things. If you add it to dishes that then need to be boiled it may separate.

* Thickened cream is stabilized with gelatine and whips more easily than pure cream.

* Double, or thick, cream has 48% butterfat and is better as a spooning cream because when it whips it turns to butter easily.

* Clotted cream is a very thick, yellowy cream that is usually eaten with warm scones or desserts.

Eton mess is a mixture of strawberries, meringue and cream. As the meringue sits in the cream it will turn gooey so, if you want your meringue crunchy, serve it straight away. You can use any soft fruit for this recipe — mango goes well, as do raspberries.

# eton mess

**meringues** 2–3 ready-made

**strawberries** 125 g (half a punnet)

**caster (superfine) sugar** $^1/_2$ teaspoon

**thick (double) cream** 125 ml ($^1/_2$ cup)

**serves** 2 **takes** 5 minutes

1 Break the meringues into pieces. Cut the strawberries into quarters and put them in a bowl with the sugar. Using a potato masher or the back of a spoon, squash them slightly so they start to become juicy. Whip the cream with a balloon or electric whisk until it is quite thick but not solid.

2 Mix everything together gently and spoon it into glasses.

This is Italy's version of trifle. You can make all the bits for this in advance and put it together just before you need it. If you don't have kirsch, use another liqueur but just remember that if you use something brown it will make the sponge brown.

# zuppa inglese

sponge or Madeira cake  2 thick slices

kirsch  2 tablespoons

raspberries  75 g (half a punnet)

blackberries  85 g (half a punnet)

caster (superfine) sugar  1 tablespoon

custard  125 ml ($^1$/2 cup)

cream  125 ml ($^1$/2 cup) lightly whipped

icing (confectioners') sugar  for dusting

serves 2   takes 15 minutes

1 Put a piece of sponge cake on each of two deep plates and brush or sprinkle it with the kirsch. Leave the kirsch to soak in for at least a minute or two.

2 Put the raspberries and blackberries in a saucepan with the caster sugar. Gently warm through over a low heat so that the sugar just melts, then leave the fruit to cool.

3 Spoon the fruit over the sponge, pour the custard on top of the fruit and, finally, dollop the cream on top and dust with icing sugar.

When mangoes are ripe and in season you can make this every day — the rest of the year you can use other soft-fleshed fruit. In the winter you can use stewed rhubarb or apple.

# mango fool

very ripe mango  1

Greek-style yoghurt  125 ml (¹/₂ cup)

cream  2 tablespoons

serves  2    takes  10 minutes

1 Take the flesh off the mango. The easiest way to do this is to slice down either side of the stone so you have 2 'cheeks'. Make crisscross cuts through the mango flesh on each cheek, almost through to the skin, then turn each cheek inside out and slice the flesh from the skin into a bowl. Cut the rest of the flesh from the stone.

2 Purée the flesh either by using a food processor, blender or Bamix, or if you don't have any of these, just mash the flesh thoroughly.

3 Put a spoonful of mango purée in the bottom of a small glass, bowl or cup, put a spoonful of yoghurt on top and then repeat. Spoon half the cream over each serving when you have used up all the mango and yoghurt. Swirl the layers together just before you eat them.

fruit

# Why fruit?

Perfect when eaten fresh, fruit can also be used in a number of sweet and savoury dishes — and it's good for you. Some fruits cook better than others and these can be made into crumbles, pies and compotes. Others are best eaten fresh in fruit salads or added to jellies.

# What to look for:

* Fruit should look fresh and healthy and skins should not be wrinkled. Berries should be undamaged and everything should feel heavy (and therefore juicy) for its size.

* If you can, hand-pick your fruit so you know that none of it is damaged. If you buy punnets of berries, check the top and bottom of the punnet so you can see if there is any mould or squashiness.

* Store fruit in the fridge if the weather is hot but eat fruit at room temperature.

# What's available?

* Stone fruits. These include peaches, nectarines, apricots and cherries. Choose ripe ones that are very slightly soft to the touch. These are good raw and cooked.

* Soft fruits. These include berries and currants. These are best when in season — strawberries always taste best in summer. Make sure none are squashed, mouldy or bruised when you buy them. Don't wash them until just before you use them. Soft fruits are best eaten raw.

* Tropical fruits. These include bananas, mangoes, pineapples, melons and all the unusual looking ones. Bananas aside, all these should have a fragrance when they are ripe — bananas will actually look ripe. Tropical fruits are best eaten raw.

* Citrus fruits. These should be heavy for their size. If you buy organic citrus fruits, they will not be evenly coloured (as they will not be if you grow your own).

* Apples and pears. Apples should be firm and pears should yield just a little. If you are cooking with apples use Granny Smiths or cooking apples for purées and Golden Delicious for tarts and pies.

Jellies are a favourite light pudding. In these ones the Champagne isn't sweetened, just the fruit. Using gelatine isn't hard once you get the hang of it — it really is no more difficult than making up a packet jelly. If you want to make more jellies just double everything.

# champagne jellies

strawberries  2 cut into quarters

blueberries  10

raspberries  8

caster (superfine) sugar  3 tablespoons

gelatine  1¹/₂ teaspoons

Champagne  2 glasses (320 ml/11 fl oz)

makes  2    takes  15 minutes plus a couple of hours to set

1 Put the berries in a small saucepan with the sugar and a tablespoon of water and heat them gently until they give off some juice and the sugar melts. Divide them between two glasses.

2 Put 2 tablespoons of water in a small bowl and sprinkle the gelatine on top of it in an even layer. Leave it to sit for a few minutes, by which time it will have soaked up some of the water and turned jellyish. Now melt the gelatine by either pouring it into a small saucepan and putting it over a low heat, or heating it gently in the microwave for a minute. Don't let it boil or it will lose its setting ability.

3 Gradually stir the Champagne into the gelatine, making sure it is well mixed.

4 Pour into the glasses, stirring once or twice. Put the glasses in the fridge to set — this should take about 2 hours.

Crumble is best served with cream or custard. You can make it with pretty much any kind of fruit but if you decide to use soft fruit such as strawberries or raspberries, remember that they will break down as they cook. Use Golden Delicious apples as they keep their shape well.

# apple crumble

apples  4

caster (superfine) sugar  2 tablespoons

lemon zest  from 1 lemon

butter  60 g (3 tablespoons)

plain (all-purpose) flour  60 g (1/2 cup)

ground cinnamon  1/2 teaspoon

serves  2    takes  1 hour 10 minutes

1 Turn the oven to 180°C (350°/Gas 4). Peel and core the apples, then cut them into chunks. Put the apple, 1 tablespoon of the sugar and the lemon zest in a small baking dish and mix them together. Dot 20 g (1 tablespoon) of butter over the top.

2 Rub the remaining butter into the flour until you have a texture that resembles coarse sand. Stir in the rest of the sugar and the cinnamon. Add a tablespoon of water and stir the crumbs together so they form bigger clumps.

3 Sprinkle the crumble mixture over the apple and bake the crumble for 1 hour, by which time the top should be browned and the juice bubbling up through the crumble. Serve with custard (page 250), ice cream or cream.

This is quite an unusual fruit salad as it has chilli and ginger in it. This gives the syrup a warmth that goes well with the lime and the sweetness of the fruit. If you prefer, you can leave it out. Serve the fruit salad with coconut ice cream if you can find it.

# spiced fruit salad

caster (superfine) sugar  60 g (1/4 cup)

ginger  2 slices

bird's eye chilli  1 cut in half

lime juice and zest  from 1 lime

fruit  a mixture of watermelon, melon, mango, banana, cherries, lychees, kiwi fruit, or anything else you fancy — enough for 2 portions

serves 2    takes 15 minutes plus chilling time

1 Put the sugar in a saucepan with 60 ml (1/4 cup) water and the ginger and chilli. Heat it until the sugar melts, then leave it to cool before adding the lime juice and zest. Take out the ginger and chilli.

2 Put your selection of fruit into a bowl and pour the syrup over it. Leave it to marinate in the fridge for 30 minutes.

3 Serve with coconut ice cream or any other kind of ice cream or sorbet.

# basics

### mayonnaise

Start with all ingredients at room temperature. Put 2 egg yolks in a deep bowl and season well. Measure 300 ml ($1^1/4$ cups) canola, groundnut (peanut) or light olive oil into a jug. Add a drop of oil to the eggs and blend with a whisk, electric beaters or blender. Repeat, then continue to add the oil, drop by drop — the mixture will start to thicken. As the mixture thickens and becomes pale and glossy, add the oil faster and faster, in a steady stream. When most of the oil has been added, add 1 to 2 tablespoons of vinegar or lemon juice. Whisk in the remaining oil and season well. Makes 375 m ($1^1/2$ cups).

### vinaigrette

Using a mortar and pestle, or the blade of a knife, crush 1 small garlic clove with a little salt to form a smooth paste. Add 1 tablespoon of good-quality vinegar and $1/2$ teaspoon of Dijon mustard and mix well. Gradually mix in 3 tablespoons of olive oil until a smooth emulsion is formed. Season with salt and pepper. Makes enough for one salad.

### custard

Beat 1 egg yolk with 1 tablespoon of caster sugar and 1 tablespoon of plain (all-purpose) flour. Heat 250 ml (1 cup) of milk until it is boiling, then stir it into the flour and sugar mixture. Mix well, making sure you have no lumps. Pour the mixture back into the saucepan and bring it to the boil again, stirring all the time so it doesn't go lumpy. It should thicken to a pouring consistency. Serves 4.

### boiled potatoes

Peel 4 large waxy potatoes, cut them into pieces and put them in a saucepan of lightly salted cold water (you could also add a sprig of mint). Bring to the boil, then simmer the potates for 15 to 20 minutes, or until they are tender. Don't boil them too hard or they'll break up. Drain, discard the mint and toss in a knob of butter if you like. Serves 4.

## mashed potatoes

Peel and chop 4 large floury potatoes. Put them in cold water and bring them to the boil. Boil until tender, drain well and put them back in the saucepan over a low heat with 2 tablespoons of hot milk, 1 tablespoon of butter and plenty of seasoning. Remove from the stove and mash with a masher (or use a potato ricer, a mouli or a wire sieve, but don't use a food processor as the mash will go gluey), then beat them with a wooden spoon until fluffy. If you like you can add more butter, a grating of nutmeg or a splash of cream. Serves 4.

## pesto

Put 2 garlic cloves in a mortar and pestle or food processor, add a pinch of salt and 55 g (2 oz) pine nuts. Pound or whizz to a paste. Gradually add 55 g (2 oz) basil leaves and pound or whizz the leaves into the base mixture. Stir in 70 g (2$^1$/$_2$ oz) grated Parmesan cheese, then gradually add 125 ml ($^1$/$_2$ cup) olive oil. Use immediately or store covered in the fridge for 1 week. If storing, cover the pesto surface with a thin layer of olive oil. Makes 250 ml (1 cup).

## boiled rice

Rinse 200 g (1 cup) of rice under cold running water until the water running away is clear, then drain well. Put the rice in a heavy-based saucepan and add enough water to come about 5 cm (2 inches) above the surface of the rice. (If you stick your index finger into the rice so it rests on the bottom of the pan, the water will come up to the second joint.) Add 1 teaspoon of salt and bring the water quickly to the boil. When it boils, cover and reduce the heat to a simmer. Cook for 15 minutes, or until the rice is just tender, then remove the saucepan from the heat and rest the rice for 10 minutes without removing the lid. Fluff the rice with a fork before serving. Serves 4.

# glossary

**balsamic vinegar**
A rich, sweet, highly fragrant vinegar made from white Trebbiano di Spagna grapes in Modena, Italy. The very best balsamic vinegars, Aceto Balsamico Tradizionale de Modena, are made of a blend of vinegars ranging from some that are up to 100 years old to younger ones (which are at least 12 years old). The commercial variety, labelled Aceto Balsamico de Modena, varies considerably in price and quality. Buy the best you can afford.

**bonito flakes**
Shavings or flakes of the Pacific bonito fish. Used as a flavouring in Japanese cooking.

**borlotti beans**
A large, slightly kidney-shaped bean. Pale pink with dark red specks. Nutty flavour. Good in soups, stews and salads. Sometimes available fresh, but more often dried or tinned are used.

**cannellini beans**
Also known as haricot beans or white kidney beans, these have a mild flavour and are an all-purpose bean.

**ciabatta**
Slipper-shaped Italian bread with a rough, open texture. Made from a very wet dough that allows large bubbles to form and gives a thin crust. Ciabatta is best eaten on the day it is bought.

**coconut milk/cream**
Both coconut cream and coconut milk are available tinned. Coconut milk is a thinner version of coconut cream. Some tins of coconut milk have a layer of coconut cream sitting on top. This cream can be scooped off if you only need a small quantity of coconut cream.

**couscous**
A fine grain processed from semolina flour. Commonly used in many countries as an accompaniment to meat and vegetable dishes, in much the same way as rice is used in Asia. Couscous is usually steamed. Instant couscous only needs to be soaked in boiling water for 5 minutes.

**crème fraîche**
Although this translates from French to mean 'fresh cream', it is actually cultured cream. It has a slightly nutty, sharp flavour without being too sour, and is higher in butterfat than sour cream so it is creamier. Unlike sour cream, it is ideal in sauces or soups because it can boil without curdling.

**dashi granules**
These granules form the basis of a basic Japanese soup stock.

**emmenthal cheese**
A hard cooked-curd cheese made from cow's milk. It has a nutty, sweetish flavour.

**feta cheese**
A soft, white cheese ripened in brine, usually sold cut into blocks. Feta cheese tastes sharp and salty. Ewe, cow and goat milk feta are all available.

**french shallot**
A small onion that grows in clusters, it has a more delicate, milder flavour than other onions.

**garam masala**
An Indian spice mix containing mostly coriander, cumin, cardamom, black pepper, cloves, cinnamon and nutmeg. There are many versions available ready-ground. Usually added as a final seasoning.

**haloumi cheese**
A salty Middle Eastern cheese, with a rubbery texture, made from ewe milk. The curd is cooked before it is matured in brine, sometimes with herbs or spices.

**harissa**
A North African spicy paste made from ground chillies and spices. It is traditionally served with couscous but is also used as a flavouring in many dishes. It is available from delicatessens in tubes or small tins.

**horseradish cream**
A hot, pungent flavouring made from grated horseradish root and cream.

**jalapeño chillies**
Pronounced hal-ap-enyo, this chilli has thick flesh and is medium in heat. Available in red or green, the skin sometimes has fine brown lines that look like cracks running along it.

**laksa paste**
A spice paste for making laksa. Several different brands are available.

**lavash bread**
A rectangular Middle Eastern flat bread that rolls up easily. Other flat bread can be substituted.

**mascarpone cheese**
A cream cheese originally from Lombardia. It is very high in fat as it is made with cream rather than milk.

**oregano**
From the same herb family as marjoram, oregano is used mainly in Greek, Italian and Middle Eastern dishes.

**palm sugar**
This is made by boiling down the sap of the palmyra or sugar palm. Soft brown sugar can be used instead if you can't buy palm sugar.

**pancetta**
Italian cured belly pork, somewhat like streaky bacon. Available in flat pieces or rolled up, and both smoked and unsmoked. It is used in recipes and is usually either sliced or cut into cubes.

**parmesan cheese**
This hard cheese is made from cow's milk. Commonly used in Italian cooking, it is often grated and added to dishes, or shaved or grated to use as a garnish. Buy small pieces of fresh Parmigiano Reggiano and grate it yourself, rather than using Parmesan that is ready-grated because this doesn't have the same fresh flavour.

**pesto**
This paste is made of basil, pine nuts, garlic, olive oil and either Parmesan or pecorino sardo cheese. Usually served as a pasta sauce, but also works well with chicken and fish.

**porcini mushrooms**
Also known as cep or boletus mushrooms, these are usually bought dried and are soaked in boiling water before use. Sometimes available fresh.

**prosciutto**
An Italian ham cured by salting, then drying in the air. After being aged for up to ten months, it is sliced very thinly. Prosciutto di Parm, the classic version, is often served as part of an antipasto platter but also used in cooking.

**risotto rice**
This is round-grained, very absorbent rice. It comes in different categories, depending on the size of the grain. Arborio, carnaroli and vialone nano are the most common types.

**saffron threads**
This expensive spice is the threadlike stigma of a violet crocus. The stigma are extracted from the flowers. Sold as threads or as a powder, the threads are preferable and it only takes a small amount to impart the distinctive flavour and colour to any dish.

**sambal oelek**
This Southeast Asian condiment is made from red chillies, vinegar and sugar, which are processed together into a paste.

**sumac**
A red berry with a sour, fruity flavour. The berry is processed into powder and used to add flavour and colour to many Middle Eastern and North African dishes.

**tahini**
Made from ground white sesame seeds, tahini is an oily paste that contributes a nutty flavour to dishes.

**tapenade**
A paste made from olives, anchovies and 'tapeno', or capers. Often spread on toast or bread as an appetizer, or used as a dip. It also makes a good instant pasta sauce.

**tofu, firm**
A reasonably solid tofu that can be used in stir-fries.

**tofu, silken**
A very soft tofu that is used for soups. It will break up if you try and stir-fry it.

**tofu puffs**
Sold as large cubes, usually in plastic bags, these are deep-fried tofu (bean curd). Crispy on the outside and spongy in the middle, they are sold in Chinese shops in the refrigerated cabinet. They can be frozen.

**tomato paste (purée)**
A concentrated paste that is a convenient way of adding flavour to soups and stews. Can be frozen in ice cube trays for ease of storage.

**tortillas, flour**
A thin unleavened bread made from maize flour or wheat flour, shaped by hand or in a tortilla press and cooked on a griddle. Tortillas can be eaten plain or wrapped around fillings.

# index

A very big thankyou to Marylouise, Katy, Ian, Wendy and Jo for making this book happen. Thanks to Kay for letting me do it, and Sifet for having a go and showing me that it works.

Published by Murdoch Books®, a division of Murdoch Magazines Pty Ltd.

Murdoch Books® Australia
GPO Box 1203, Sydney NSW 1045
Phone: + 61 (0) 2 4352 7000    Fax: + 61 (0) 2 4352 7026

Murdoch Books UK Limited
Ferry House, 51–57 Lacy Road, Putney, London SW15 1PR
Phone: + 44 (0) 20 8355 1480    Fax: + 44 (0) 20 8355 1499

The publisher would like to thank the following for their assistance with this book:
AEG Kitchen Appliances; Breville Holdings Pty Ltd; Füritechnics Pty Ltd.

Chief Executive:  Juliet Rogers

Publisher:  Kay Scarlett

Production Manager:  Kylie Kirkwood

Art Direction and Design:  Marylouise Brammer
Photographer:  Ian Hofstetter
Stylist:  Katy Holder    Stylist's Assistant:  Jo Glynn
Food Editor: Lulu Grimes
Editorial Director: Diana Hill    Editor: Wendy Stephen

Printed by Toppan Printing Hong Kong Co. Ltd. PRINTED IN CHINA

National Library of Australia Cataloguing-in-Publication Data
ISBN 086411 859 7.  1. Cookery.  I . Title.  641.5

NOTE: We have used 20 ml tablespoon measures. If you are using a 15 ml tablespoon, for most recipes the difference will not be noticeable. However, for recipes using small amounts of flour and cornflour, add an extra teaspoon for each tablespoon specified.

IMPORTANT: Those who might be at risk from the effects of salmonella poisoning (the elderly, pregnant women, young children and those suffering from immune deficiency diseases) should consult their GP with any concerns about eating raw eggs.